BURMESE
VOCABULARY

FOR ENGLISH SPEAKERS

ENGLISH-
BURMESE

The most useful words
To expand your lexicon and sharpen
your language skills

3000 words

Burmese vocabulary for English speakers - 3000 words
By Andrey Taranov

T&P Books vocabularies are intended for helping you learn, memorize and review foreign words. The dictionary is divided into themes, covering all major spheres of everyday activities, business, science, culture, etc.

The process of learning words using T&P Books' theme-based dictionaries gives you the following advantages:

- Correctly grouped source information predetermines success at subsequent stages of word memorization
- Availability of words derived from the same root allowing memorization of word units (rather than separate words)
- Small units of words facilitate the process of establishing associative links needed for consolidation of vocabulary
- Level of language knowledge can be estimated by the number of learned words

T&P Books Publishing
www.tpbooks.com

ISBN: 978-1-83955-045-4

This book is also available in E-book formats.
Please visit www.tpbooks.com or the major online bookstores.

BURMESE VOCABULARY
for English speakers

T&P Books vocabularies are intended to help you learn, memorize, and review foreign words. The vocabulary contains over 3000 commonly used words arranged thematically.

- Vocabulary contains the most commonly used words
- Recommended as an addition to any language course
- Meets the needs of beginners and advanced learners of foreign languages
- Convenient for daily use, revision sessions, and self-testing activities
- Allows you to assess your vocabulary

Special features of the vocabulary

- Words are organized according to their meaning, not alphabetically
- Words are presented in three columns to facilitate the reviewing and self-testing processes
- Words in groups are divided into small blocks to facilitate the learning process
- The vocabulary offers a convenient and simple transcription of each foreign word

The vocabulary has 101 topics including:

Basic Concepts, Numbers, Colors, Months, Seasons, Units of Measurement, Clothing & Accessories, Food & Nutrition, Restaurant, Family Members, Relatives, Character, Feelings, Emotions, Diseases, City, Town, Sightseeing, Shopping, Money, House, Home, Office, Working in the Office, Import & Export, Marketing, Job Search, Sports, Education, Computer, Internet, Tools, Nature, Countries, Nationalities and more ...

TABLE OF CONTENTS

PRONUNCIATION GUIDE

Comments

Transcription used in this book - the Myanmar Language Commission Transcription System (MLCTS)
A description of this system can be found here:
https://en.wiktionary.org/wiki/Wiktionary:Burmese_transliteration
https://en.wikipedia.org/wiki/MLC_Transcription_System

ABBREVIATIONS
used in the vocabulary

English abbreviations

ab.	-	about
adj	-	adjective
adv	-	adverb
anim.	-	animate
as adj	-	attributive noun used as adjective
e.g.	-	for example
etc.	-	et cetera
fam.	-	familiar
fem.	-	feminine
form.	-	formal
inanim.	-	inanimate
masc.	-	masculine
math	-	mathematics
mil.	-	military
n	-	noun
pl	-	plural
pron.	-	pronoun
sb	-	somebody
sing.	-	singular
sth	-	something
v aux	-	auxiliary verb
vi	-	intransitive verb
vi, vt	-	intransitive, transitive verb
vt	-	transitive verb

BASIC CONCEPTS

1. Pronouns

I, me	ကျွန်ုပ်	kjunou'
you	သင်	thin
he	သူ	thu
she	သူမ	thu ma.
it	၎င်း	jin:
we	ကျွန်ုပ်တို့	kjunou' tou.
we (masc.)	ကျွန်တော်တို့	kjun do. dou.
we (fem.)	ကျွန်မတို့	kjun ma. tou.
you (to a group)	သင်တို့	thin dou.
you (polite, sing.)	သင်	thin
you (polite, pl)	သင်တို့	thin dou.
they (masc.)	သူတို့	thu dou.
they (fem.)	သူမတို့	thu ma. dou.

2. Greetings. Salutations

Hello! (fam.)	မင်္ဂလာပါ	min ga. la ba
Hello! (form.)	မင်္ဂလာပါ	min ga. la ba
Good morning!	မင်္ဂလာနံနက်ခင်းပါ	min ga. la nan ne' gin: ba
Good afternoon!	မင်္ဂလာနေ့လယ်ခင်းပါ	min ga. la nei. le gin: ba
Good evening!	မင်္ဂလာညနေခင်းပါ	min ga. la nja nei gin: ba
to say hello	နှုတ်ဆက်သည်	hnou' hsei' te
Hi! (hello)	ဟိုင်း	hain:
greeting (n)	ဟလို	ha. lou
to greet (vt)	နှုတ်ဆက်သည်	hnou' hsei' te
How are you?	နေကောင်းလား	nei gaun: la:
How are you? (form.)	နေကောင်းပါသလား	nei gaun: ba dha la:
How are you? (fam.)	အဆင်ပြေလား	ahsin bjei la:
What's new?	ဘာထူးသေးလဲ	ba du: dei: le:
Bye-Bye! Goodbye!	နောက်မှတွေ့ကြမယ်	nau' hma. dwei. gja. me
Goodbye!	ဂွတ်ဘိုင်	gu' bain
Bye!	တာ့တာ	ta. da
See you soon!	မကြာခင်ပြန်ဆုံကြမယ်	ma gja. gin bjan zoun gja. me
Farewell!	နှုတ်ဆက်ပါတယ်	hnou' hsei' pa de

to say goodbye	နှုတ်ဆက်သည်	hnou' hsei' te
So long!	တာ့တာ	ta. da
Thank you!	ကျေးဇူးတင်ပါတယ်	kjei: zu: din ba de
Thank you very much!	ကျေးဇူးအများ ကြီးတင်ပါတယ်	kjei: zu: amja: kji: din ba de
You're welcome	ရပါတယ်	ja. ba de
Don't mention it!	ကိစ္စမရှိပါဘူး	kei. sa ma. shi. ba bu:
It was nothing	ရပါတယ်	ja. ba de
Excuse me! (fam.)	ဆောရီးနော်	hso: ji: no:
Excuse me! (form.)	တောင်းပန်ပါတယ်	thaun: ban ba de
to excuse (forgive)	ခွင့်လွှတ်သည်	khwin. hlu' te
to apologize (vi)	တောင်းပန်သည်	thaun: ban de
My apologies	တောင်းပန်ပါတယ်	thaun: ban ba de
I'm sorry!	ခွင့်လွှတ်ပါ	khwin. hlu' pa
to forgive (vt)	ခွင့်လွှတ်သည်	khwin. hlu' te
It's okay! (that's all right)	ကိစ္စမရှိပါဘူး	kei. sa ma. shi. ba bu:
please (adv)	ကျေးဇူးပြု၍	kjei: zu: pju. i.
Don't forget!	မမေ့ပါနဲ့	ma. mei. ba ne.
Certainly!	ရတာပေါ့	ja. da bo.
Of course not!	မဟုတ်တာသေချာတယ်	ma hou' ta dhei gja de
Okay! (I agree)	သဘောတူတယ်	dhabo: tu de
That's enough!	တော်ပြီ	to bji

3. Questions

Who?	ဘယ်သူလဲ	be dhu le:
What?	ဘာလဲ	ba le:
Where? (at, in)	ဘယ်မှာလဲ	be hma le:
Where (to)?	ဘယ်ကိုလဲ	be gou le:
From where?	ဘယ်ကလဲ	be ga. le:
When?	ဘယ်တော့လဲ	be do. le:
Why? (What for?)	ဘာအတွက်လဲ	ba atwe' le:
Why? (~ are you crying?)	ဘာကြောင့်လဲ	ba gjaun. le:
What for?	ဘာအတွက်လဲ	ba atwe' le:
How? (in what way)	ဘယ်လိုလဲ	be lau le:
What? (What kind of ...?)	ဘယ်လိုမျိုးလဲ	be lau mjou: le:
Which?	ဘယ်ဟာလဲ	be ha le:
To whom?	ဘယ်သူ့ကိုလဲ	be dhu. gou le:
About whom?	ဘယ်သူ့အကြောင်းလဲ	be dhu. kjaun: le:
About what?	ဘာအကြောင်းလဲ	ba akjain: le:
With whom?	ဘယ်သူ့နဲ့လဲ	be dhu ne. le:
How many? How much?	ဘယ်လောက်လဲ	be lau' le:
Whose?	ဘယ်သူ့	be dhu.

4. Prepositions

with (accompanied by)	နဲ့အတူ	ne. atu
without	မပါဘဲ	ma. ba be:
to (indicating direction)	သို့	thou.
about (talking ~ ...)	အကြောင်း	akjaun:
before (in time)	မတိုင်မီ	ma. dain mi
in front of ...	ရှေ့မှာ	shei. hma
under (beneath, below)	အောက်မှာ	au' hma
above (over)	အပေါ်မှာ	apo hma
on (atop)	အပေါ်	apo
from (off, out of)	မှ	hma.
of (made from)	ဖြင့်	hpjin.
in (e.g., ~ ten minutes)	နောက်	nau'
over (across the top of)	ဖြတ်လျက်	hpja' lje'

5. Function words. Adverbs. Part 1

Where? (at, in)	ဘယ်မှာလဲ	be hma le:
here (adv)	ဒီမှာ	di hma
there (adv)	ဟိုမှာ	hou hma.
somewhere (to be)	တစ်နေရာရာမှာ	ti' nei ja ja hma
nowhere (not in any place)	ဘယ်မှာမှ	be hma hma.
by (near, beside)	နားမှာ	na: hma
by the window	ပြတင်းပေါက်နားမှာ	badin: pau' hna: hma
Where (to)?	ဘယ်ကိုလဲ	be gou le:
here (e.g., come ~!)	ဒီဘက်ကို	di be' kou
there (e.g., to go ~)	ဟိုဘက်ကို	hou be' kou
from here (adv)	ဒီဘက်မှ	di be' hma
from there (adv)	ဟိုဘက်မှ	hou be' hma.
close (adv)	နီးသည်	ni: de
far (adv)	အဝေးမှာ	awei: hma
near (e.g., ~ Paris)	နားမှာ	na: hma
nearby (adv)	ဘေးမှာ	bei: hma
not far (adv)	မနီးမဝေး	ma. ni ma. wei:
left (adj)	ဘယ်	be
on the left	ဘယ်ဘက်မှာ	be be' hma
to the left	ဘယ်ဘက်	be be'
right (adj)	ညာဘက်	nja be'
on the right	ညာဘက်မှာ	nja be' hma

to the right	ညာဘက်	nja be'
in front (adv)	ရှေ့မှာ	shei. hma
front (as adj)	ရှေ့	shei.
ahead (the kids ran ~)	ရှေ့	shei.

behind (adv)	နောက်မှာ	nau' hma
from behind	နောက်က	nau' ka.
back (towards the rear)	နောက်	nau'

| middle | အလယ် | ale |
| in the middle | အလယ်မှာ | ale hma |

at the side	ဘေးမှာ	bei: hma
everywhere (adv)	နေရာတိုင်းမှာ	nei ja dain: hma
around (in all directions)	ပတ်လည်မှာ	pa' le hma

from inside	အထဲမှ	a hte: hma.
somewhere (to go)	တစ်နေရာရာကို	ti' nei ja ja gou
straight (directly)	တိုက်ရိုက်	tai' jai'
back (e.g., come ~)	အပြန်	apjan

| from anywhere | တစ်နေရာရာမှ | ti' nei ja ja hma. |
| from somewhere | တစ်နေရာရာမှ | ti' nei ja ja hma. |

firstly (adv)	ပထမအနေဖြင့်	pahtama. anei gjin.
secondly (adv)	ဒုတိယအနေဖြင့်	du. di. ja. anei bjin.
thirdly (adv)	တတိယအနေဖြင့်	tati. ja. anei bjin.

suddenly (adv)	မတော်တဆ	ma. do da. za.
at first (in the beginning)	အစမှာ	asa. hma
for the first time	ပထမဆုံး	pahtama. zoun:
long before ...	မတိုင်ခင် အတော် လေး အလိုက	ma. dain gin ato lei: alou ga.

| anew (over again) | အသစ်တဖန် | athi' da. ban |
| for good (adv) | အမြဲတမ်း | amje: dan: |

never (adv)	ဘယ်တော့မှ	be do hma.
again (adv)	တဖန်	tahpan
now (at present)	အခုတော့	akhu dau.
often (adv)	ခဏခဏ	khana. khana.
then (adv)	ထိုသို့ဖြစ်လျှင်	htou dhou. bji' shin
urgently (quickly)	အမြန်	aman
usually (adv)	ပုံမှန်	poun hman

by the way, ...	စကားမစပ်	zaga: ma. za'
possibly	ဖြစ်နိုင်သည်	hpjin nain de
probably (adv)	ဖြစ်နိုင်သည်	hpji' nein de
maybe (adv)	ဖြစ်နိုင်သည်	hpji' nein de
besides ...	ဒါ့အပြင်	da. apjin
that's why ...	ဒါကြောင့်	da. gjaun.
in spite of ...	သော်လည်း	tho lei:
thanks to ...	ကြောင့်	kjaun.

13

what (pron.)	ဘာ	ba
that (conj.)	ဟု	hu
something	တစ်ခုခု	ti' khu. gu.
anything (something)	တစ်ခုခု	ti' khu. gu.
nothing	ဘာမှ	ba hma.
who (pron.)	ဘယ်သူ	be dhu.
someone	တစ်ယောက်ယောက်	ti' jau' jau'
somebody	တစ်ယောက်ယောက်	ti' jau' jau'
nobody	ဘယ်သူမှ	be dhu hma.
nowhere (a voyage to ~)	ဘယ်ကိုမှ	be gou hma.
nobody's	ဘယ်သူမှမပိုင်သော	be dhu hma ma. bain de.
somebody's	တစ်ယောက်ယောက်ရဲ့	ti' jau' jau' je.
so (I'm ~ glad)	ဒီလို	di lou
also (as well)	ထို့ပြင်လည်း	htou. bjin le:
too (as well)	လည်းဘဲ	le: be:

6. Function words. Adverbs. Part 2

Why?	ဘာကြောင့်လဲ	ba gjaun. le:
for some reason	တစ်ခုခုကြောင့်	ti' khu. gu. gjaun.
because ...	အဘယ်ကြောင့်ဆိုသော်	abe gjo:n. zou dho
for some purpose	တစ်ခုခုအတွက်	ti' khu. gu. atwe'
and	နှင့်	hnin.
or	သို့မဟုတ်	thou. ma. hou'
but	ဒါပေမဲ့	da bei me.
for (e.g., ~ me)	အတွက်	atwe'
too (~ many people)	အလွန်	alun
only (exclusively)	သာ	tha
exactly (adv)	အတိအကျ	ati. akja.
about (more or less)	ခန့်	khan.
approximately (adv)	ခန့်မှန်းခြေအားဖြင့်	khan hman: gjei a: bjin.
approximate (adj)	ခန့်မှန်းခြေဖြစ်သော	khan hman: gjei bji' te.
almost (adv)	နီးပါး	ni: ba:
the rest	ကျန်သော	kjan de.
the other (second)	တခြားသော	tacha: de.
other (different)	အခြားသော	apja: de.
each (adj)	တိုင်း	tain:
any (no matter which)	မဆို	ma. zou
many (adj)	အမြောက်အမြား	amjau' amja:
much (adv)	အများကြီး	amja: gji:
many, much (a lot of)	အမြောက်အမြား	amjau' amja:
many people	များစွာသော	mja: zwa de.
all (everyone)	အားလုံး	a: loun:

in return for ...	အစား	asa:
in exchange (adv)	အစား	asa:
by hand (made)	လက်ဖြင့်	le' hpjin.
hardly (negative opinion)	ဖြစ်နိုင်ခြေ နည်းသသည်	hpji' nain gjei ni: de
probably (adv)	ဖြစ်နိုင်သည်	hpji' nein de
on purpose (intentionally)	တမင်	tamin
by accident (adv)	အမှတ်တမဲ့	ahma' ta. me.
very (adv)	သိပ်	thei'
for example (adv)	ဥပမာအားဖြင့်	upama a: bjin.
between	ကြား	kja:
among	ကြားထဲတွင်	ka: de: dwin:
so much (such a lot)	ဒီလောက်	di lau'
especially (adv)	အထူးသဖြင့်	a htu: dha. hjin.

NUMBERS. MISCELLANEOUS

7. Cardinal numbers. Part 1

0 zero	သုည	thoun nja.
1 one	တစ်	ti'
2 two	နှစ်	hni'
3 three	သုံး	thoun:
4 four	လေး	lei:
5 five	ငါး	nga:
6 six	ခြောက်	chau'
7 seven	ခုနစ်	khun hni'
8 eight	ရှစ်	shi'
9 nine	ကိုး	kou:
10 ten	တစ်ဆယ်	ti' hse
11 eleven	တစ်ဆယ့်တစ်	ti' hse. ti'
12 twelve	တစ်ဆယ်နှစ်	ti' hse. hni'
13 thirteen	တစ်ဆယ့်သုံး	ti' hse. thoun:
14 fourteen	တစ်ဆယ့်လေး	ti' hse. lei:
15 fifteen	တစ်ဆယ့်ငါး	ti' hse. nga:
16 sixteen	တစ်ဆယ့်ခြောက်	ti' hse. khau'
17 seventeen	တစ်ဆယ့်ခုနစ်	ti' hse. khu ni'
18 eighteen	တစ်ဆယ့်ရှစ်	ti' hse. shi'
19 nineteen	တစ်ဆယ့်ကိုး	ti' hse. gou:
20 twenty	နှစ်ဆယ်	hni' hse
21 twenty-one	နှစ်ဆယ့်တစ်	hni' hse. ti'
22 twenty-two	နှစ်ဆယ့်နှစ်	hni' hse. hni'
23 twenty-three	နှစ်ဆယ့်သုံး	hni' hse. thuan:
30 thirty	သုံးဆယ်	thoun: ze
31 thirty-one	သုံးဆယ့်တစ်	thoun: ze. di'
32 thirty-two	သုံးဆယ့်နှစ်	thoun: ze. hni'
33 thirty-three	သုံးဆယ့်သုံး	thoun: ze. dhoun:
40 forty	လေးဆယ်	lei: hse
41 forty-one	လေးဆယ့်တစ်	lei: hse. ti'
42 forty-two	လေးဆယ့်နှစ်	lei: hse. hni'
43 forty-three	လေးဆယ့်သုံး	lei: hse. thaun:
50 fifty	ငါးဆယ်	nga: ze
51 fifty-one	ငါးဆယ့်တစ်	nga: ze di'
52 fifty-two	ငါးဆယ့်နှစ်	nga: ze hni'

53	fifty-three	ငါးဆယ့်သုံး	nga: ze dhoun:
60	sixty	ခြောက်ဆယ်	chau' hse
61	sixty-one	ခြောက်ဆယ့်တစ်	chau' hse. di'
62	sixty-two	ခြောက်ဆယ့်နှစ်	chau' hse. hni'
63	sixty-three	ခြောက်ဆယ့်သုံး	chau' hse. dhoun:
70	seventy	ခုနစ်ဆယ်	khun hni' hse.
71	seventy-one	ခုနစ်ဆယ့်တစ်	qunxcy•tx
72	seventy-two	ခုနစ်ဆယ့်နှစ်	khun hni' hse. hni
73	seventy-three	ခုနစ်ဆယ့်သုံး	khu. ni' hse. dhoun:
80	eighty	ရှစ်ဆယ်	shi' hse
81	eighty-one	ရှစ်ဆယ့်တစ်	shi' hse. ti'
82	eighty-two	ရှစ်ဆယ့်နှစ်	shi' hse. hni'
83	eighty-three	ရှစ်ဆယ့်သုံး	shi' hse. dhun:
90	ninety	ကိုးဆယ်	kou: hse
91	ninety-one	ကိုးဆယ့်တစ်	kou: hse. ti'
92	ninety-two	ကိုးဆယ့်နှစ်	kou: hse. hni'
93	ninety-three	ကိုးဆယ့်သုံး	kou: hse. dhaun:

8. Cardinal numbers. Part 2

100	one hundred	တစ်ရာ	ti' ja
200	two hundred	နှစ်ရာ	hni' ja
300	three hundred	သုံးရာ	thoun: ja
400	four hundred	လေးရာ	lei: ja
500	five hundred	ငါးရာ	nga: ja
600	six hundred	ခြောက်ရာ	chau' ja
700	seven hundred	ခုနစ်ရာ	khun hni' ja
800	eight hundred	ရှစ်ရာ	shi' ja
900	nine hundred	ကိုးရာ	kou: ja
1000	one thousand	တစ်ထောင်	ti' htaun
2000	two thousand	နှစ်ထောင်	hni' taun
3000	three thousand	သုံးထောင်	thoun: daun
10000	ten thousand	တစ်သောင်း	ti' thaun:
	one hundred thousand	တစ်သိန်း	ti' thein:
	million	တစ်သန်း	ti' than:
	billion	ဘီလီယံ	bi li jan

9. Ordinal numbers

first (adj)	ပထမ	pahtama.
second (adj)	ဒုတိယ	du. di. ja.
third (adj)	တတိယ	tati. ja.
fourth (adj)	စတုတ္ထ	zadou' hta.

17

fifth (adj)	ပဉ္စမ	pjin sama.
sixth (adj)	ဆဋ္ဌမ	hsa. htama.
seventh (adj)	သတ္တမ	tha' tama.
eighth (adj)	အဋ္ဌမ	a' htama.
ninth (adj)	နဝမ	na. wa. ma.
tenth (adj)	ဒသမ	da dha ma

COLOURS. UNITS OF MEASUREMENT

color	အရောင်	ajaun
shade (tint)	အသွေးအဆင်း	athwei: ahsin:
hue	အရောင်အသွေး	ajaun athwei:
rainbow	သက်တံ	the' tan
white (adj)	အဖြူရောင်	ahpju jaun
black (adj)	အနက်ရောင်	ane' jaun
gray (adj)	မဲရောင်	khe: jaun
green (adj)	အစိမ်းရောင်	asain: jaun
yellow (adj)	အဝါရောင်	awa jaun
red (adj)	အနီရောင်	ani jaun
blue (adj)	အပြာရောင်	apja jaun
light blue (adj)	အပြာနုရောင်	apja nu. jaun
pink (adj)	ပန်းရောင်	pan: jaun
orange (adj)	လိမ္မော်ရောင်	limmo jaun
violet (adj)	ခရမ်းရောင်	khajan: jaun
brown (adj)	အညိုရောင်	anjou jaun
golden (adj)	ရွှေရောင်	shwei jaun
silvery (adj)	ငွေရောင်	ngwei jaun
beige (adj)	ဝါညိုနုရောင်	wa njou nu. jaun
cream (adj)	နို့ခဲရောင်	nou. hni' jaun
turquoise (adj)	စိမ်းပြာရောင်	sein: bja jaun
cherry red (adj)	ချယ်ရီရောင်	che ji jaun
lilac (adj)	ခရမ်းဖျော့ရောင်	khajan: bjo. jaun
crimson (adj)	ကြက်သွေးရောင်	kje' thwei: jaun
light (adj)	အရောင်ဖျော့သော	ajaun bjo. de.
dark (adj)	အရောင်ရင့်သော	ajaun jin. de.
bright, vivid (adj)	တောက်ပသော	tau' pa. de.
colored (pencils)	အရောင်ရှိသော	ajaun shi. de.
color (e.g., ~ film)	ရောင်စုံ	jau' soun
black-and-white (adj)	အဖြူအမည်း	ahpju ame:
plain (one-colored)	တစ်ရောင်တည်းရှိသော	ti' jaun te: shi. de.
multicolored (adj)	အရောင်စုံသော	ajaun zoun de.

11. Units of measurement

weight	အလေးချိန်	alei: gjein
length	အရှည်	ashei
width	အကျယ်	akje
height	အမြင့်	amjin.
depth	အနက်	ane'
volume	ထုထည်	du. de
area	အကျယ်အဝန်း	akje awun:
gram	ဂရမ်	ga ran
milligram	မိလီဂရမ်	mi li ga. jan
kilogram	ကီလိုဂရမ်	ki lou ga jan
ton	တန်	tan
pound	ပေါင်	paun
ounce	အောင်စ	aun sa.
meter	မီတာ	mi ta
millimeter	မိလီမီတာ	mi li mi ta
centimeter	စင်တီမီတာ	sin ti mi ta
kilometer	ကီလိုမီတာ	ki lou mi ta
mile	မိုင်	main
inch	လက်မ	le' ma
foot	ပေ	pei
yard	ကိုက်	kou'
square meter	စတုရန်းမီတာ	satu. jan: mi ta
hectare	ဟက်တာ	he' ta
liter	လီတာ	li ta
degree	ဒီဂရီ	di ga ji
volt	ဗို့	boi.
ampere	အမ်ပီယာ	an bi ja
horsepower	မြင်းကောင်ရေအား	mjin: gaun jei a:
quantity	အရေအတွက်	ajei adwe'
a little bit of ...	နည်းနည်း	ne: ne:
half	တစ်ဝက်	ti' we'
dozen	ဒါဇင်	da zin
piece (item)	ခု	khu.
size	အတိုင်းအတာ	atain: ata
scale (map ~)	စကေး	sakei:
minimal (adj)	အနည်းဆုံး	ane: zoun
the smallest (adj)	အသေးဆုံး	athei: zoun:
medium (adj)	အလယ်အလတ်	ale ala'
maximal (adj)	အများဆုံး	amja: zoun:
the largest (adj)	အကြီးဆုံး	akji: zoun:

12. Containers

canning jar (glass ~)	ဖန်ဘူး	hpan bu:
can	သံဘူး	than bu:
bucket	ရေပုံး	jei boun:
barrel	စည်ပိုင်း	si bain:
wash basin (e.g., plastic ~)	ဇလုံ	za loun
tank (100L water ~)	သံစည်	than zi
hip flask	အရက်ပုလင်းပြား	aje' pu lin: pja:
jerrycan	ဓာတ်ဆီပုံး	da' hsi boun:
tank (e.g., tank car)	တိုင်ကီ	tain ki
mug	မတ်ခွက်	ma' khwe'
cup (of coffee, etc.)	ခွက်	khwe'
saucer	အောက်ခံပန်းကန်ပြား	au' khan ban: kan pja:
glass (tumbler)	ဖန်ခွက်	hpan gwe'
wine glass	ဝိုင်ခွက်	wain gwe'
stock pot (soup pot)	ပေါင်းအိုး	paun: ou:
bottle (~ of wine)	ပုလင်း	palin:
neck (of the bottle, etc.)	ပုလင်းလည်ပင်း	palin: le bin:
carafe (decanter)	ဖန်ချိုင့်	hpan gjain.
pitcher	ကရား	kaja:
vessel (container)	အိုးခွက်	ou: khwe'
pot (crock, stoneware ~)	မြေအိုး	mjei ou:
vase	ပန်းအိုး	pan: ou:
flacon, bottle (perfume ~)	ပုလင်း	palin:
vial, small bottle	ပုလင်းကလေး	palin: galei:
tube (of toothpaste)	ဘူး	bu:
sack (bag)	ဂုံနီအိတ်	goun ni ei'
bag (paper ~, plastic ~)	အိတ်	ei'
pack (of cigarettes, etc.)	ဘူး	bu:
box (e.g., shoebox)	စက္ကူဘူး	se' ku bu:
crate	သေတ္တာ	thi' ta
basket	တောင်း	taun:

MAIN VERBS

13. The most important verbs. Part 1

to advise (vt)	အကြံပေးသည်	akjan bei: de
to agree (say yes)	သဘောတူသည်	dhabo: tu de
to answer (vi, vt)	ဖြေသည်	hpjei de
to apologize (vi)	တောင်းပန်သည်	thaun: ban de
to arrive (vi)	ရောက်သည်	jau' te
to ask (~ oneself)	မေးသည်	mei: de
to ask (~ sb to do sth)	တောင်းဆိုသည်	taun: hsou: de
to be (~ a teacher)	ဖြစ်သည်	hpji' te
to be (~ on a diet)	ဖြစ်နေသည်	hpji' nei de
to be afraid	ကြောက်သည်	kjau' te
to be hungry	ဗိုက်ဆာသည်	bai' hsa de
to be interested in …	စိတ်ဝင်စားသည်	sei' win za: de
to be needed	အလိုရှိသည်	alou' shi. de
to be surprised	အံ့ဩသည်	an. o. de
to be thirsty	ရေဆာသည်	jei za de
to begin (vt)	စတင်သည်	sa. tin de
to belong to …	ပိုင်ဆိုင်သည်	pain zain de
to boast (vi)	ကြွားသည်	kjwa: de
to break (split into pieces)	ချက်ဆီးသည်	hpje' hsi: de
to call (~ for help)	ခေါ်သည်	kho de
can (v aux)	တတ်နိုင်သည်	ta' nain de
to catch (vt)	ဖမ်းသည်	hpan: de
to change (vt)	ပြောင်းလဲသည်	pjaun: le: de
to choose (select)	ရွေးသည်	jwei: de
to come down (the stairs)	ဆင်းသည်	hsin: de
to compare (vt)	နှိုင်းယှဉ်သည်	hnain: shin de
to complain (vi, vt)	တိုင်ပြောသည်	tain bjo: de
to confuse (mix up)	ရောထွေးသည်	jo: dwei: de
to continue (vt)	ဆက်လုပ်သည်	hse' lou' te
to control (vt)	ထိန်းချုပ်သည်	htein: gjou' te
to cook (dinner)	ချက်ပြုတ်သည်	che' pjou' te
to cost (vt)	ကုန်ကျသည်	koun kja de
to count (add up)	ရေတွက်သည်	jei dwe' te
to count on …	အားကိုးသည်	a: kou: de
to create (vt)	ဖန်တီးသည်	hpan di: de
to cry (weep)	ငိုသည်	ngou de

14. The most important verbs. Part 2

to deceive (vi, vt)	လိမ်ပြောသည်	lain bjo: de
to decorate (tree, street)	အလှဆင်သည်	ahla. zin dhe
to defend (a country, etc.)	ကာကွယ်သည်	ka gwe de
to demand (request firmly)	တိုက်တွန်းသည်	tai' tun: de
to dig (vt)	တူးသည်	tu: de

to discuss (vt)	ဆွေးနွေးသည်	hswe: nwe: de
to do (vt)	ပြုလုပ်သည်	pju. lou' te
to doubt (have doubts)	သံသယဖြစ်သည်	than thaja. bji' te
to drop (let fall)	ဖြုတ်ချသည်	hpjou' cha. de
to enter (room, house, etc.)	ဝင်သည်	win de

to excuse (forgive)	ခွင့်လွှတ်သည်	khwin. hlu' te
to exist (vi)	တည်ရှိသည်	ti shi. de
to expect (foresee)	ကြိုမြင်သည်	kjou mjin de

to explain (vt)	ရှင်းပြသည်	shin: bja. de
to fall (vi)	ကျဆင်းသည်	kja zin: de

to find (vt)	ရှာတွေ့သည်	sha dwei. de
to finish (vt)	ပြီးသည်	pji: de
to fly (vi)	ပျံသန်းသည်	pjan dan: de

to follow ... (come after)	လိုက်သည်	lai' te
to forget (vi, vt)	မေ့သည်	mei. de

to forgive (vt)	ခွင့်လွှတ်သည်	khwin. hlu' te
to give (vt)	ပေးသည်	pei: de

to give a hint	အရိပ်အမြွက်ပေးသည်	aji' ajmwe' pei: de
to go (on foot)	သွားသည်	thwa: de

to go for a swim	ရေကူးသည်	jei ku: de
to go out (for dinner, etc.)	ထွက်သည်	htwe' te
to guess (the answer)	မှန်းဆသည်	hman za de

to have (vt)	ရှိသည်	shi. de
to have breakfast	နံနက်စာစားသည်	nan ne' za za: de
to have dinner	ညစာစားသည်	nja. za za: de

to have lunch	နေ့လယ်စာစားသည်	nei. le za za de
to hear (vt)	ကြားသည်	ka: de

to help (vt)	ကူညီသည်	ku nji de
to hide (vt)	ဖုံးကွယ်သည်	hpoun: gwe de
to hope (vi, vt)	မျှော်လင့်သည်	hmjo. lin. de
to hunt (vi, vt)	အမဲလိုက်သည်	ame: lai' de
to hurry (vi)	လောသည်	lo de

15. The most important verbs. Part 3

to inform (vt)	အကြောင်းကြားသည်	akjaun: kja: de
to insist (vi, vt)	တိုက်တွန်းပြောဆိုသည်	tou' tun: bjo: zou de
to insult (vt)	စော်ကားသည်	so ga: de
to invite (vt)	ဖိတ်သည်	hpi' de
to joke (vi)	စနောက်သည်	sanau' te
to keep (vt)	ထိန်းထားသည်	htein: da: de
to keep silent, to hush	နှုတ်ဆိတ်သည်	hnou' hsei' te
to kill (vt)	သတ်သည်	tha' te
to know (sb)	သိသည်	thi. de
to know (sth)	သိသည်	thi. de
to laugh (vi)	ရယ်သည်	je de
to liberate (city, etc.)	လွတ်မြောက်စေသည်	lu' mjau' sei de
to like (I like …)	ကြိုက်သည်	kjai' de
to look for … (search)	ရှာသည်	sha de
to love (sb)	ချစ်သည်	chi' te
to make a mistake	မှားသည်	hma: de
to manage, to run	စွန့်ကြားသည်	hnjun gja: de
to mean (signify)	ဆိုလိုသည်	hsou lou de
to mention (talk about)	ဖော်ပြသည်	hpjo bja. de
to miss (school, etc.)	ပျက်ကွက်သည်	pje' kwe' te
to notice (see)	သတိထားမိသည်	dhadi. da: mi. de
to object (vi, vt)	ငြင်းသည်	njin: de
to observe (see)	စောင့်ကြည့်သည်	saun. gji. de
to open (vt)	ဖွင့်သည်	hpwin. de
to order (meal, etc.)	မှာသည်	hma de
to order (mil.)	အမိန့်ပေးသည်	amin. bei: de
to own (possess)	ပိုင်ဆိုင်သည်	pain zain de
to participate (vi)	ပါဝင်သည်	pa win de
to pay (vi, vt)	ပေးချေသည်	pei: gjei de
to permit (vt)	ခွင့်ပြုသည်	khwin bju. de
to plan (vt)	စီစဉ်သည်	si zin de
to play (children)	ကစားသည်	gaza: de
to pray (vi, vt)	ရှိခိုးသည်	shi. gou: de
to prefer (vt)	ပို၍ကြိုက်သည်	pou gjai' te
to promise (vt)	ကတိပေးသည်	gadi pei: de
to pronounce (vt)	အသံထွက်သည်	athan dwe' te
to propose (vt)	အဆိုပြုသည်	ahsou bju. de
to punish (vt)	အပြစ်ပေးသည်	apja' pei: de

16. The most important verbs. Part 4

to read (vi, vt)	ဖတ်သည်	hpa' te
to recommend (vt)	အကြံပြုထောက်ခံသည်	akjan pju htau' khan de

to refuse (vi, vt)	ြခင်းဆန်သည်	njin: zan de
to regret (be sorry)	နောင်တရသည်	naun da. ja. de
to rent (sth from sb)	ငှားသည်	hnga: de
to repeat (say again)	ထပ်လုပ်သည်	hta' lou' te
to reserve, to book	မှာသည်	hma de
to run (vi)	ပြေးသည်	pjei: de
to save (rescue)	ကယ်ဆယ်သည်	ke ze de
to say (~ thank you)	ပြောသည်	pjo: de
to scold (vt)	ဆူသည်	hsu. de
to see (vt)	မြင်သည်	mjin de
to sell (vt)	ရောင်းသည်	jaun: de
to send (vt)	ပို့သည်	pou. de
to shoot (vi)	ပစ်သည်	pi' te
to shout (vi)	အော်သည်	o de
to show (vt)	ြပသည်	pja. de
to sign (document)	လက်မှတ်ထိုးသည်	le' hma' htou: de
to sit down (vi)	ထိုင်သည်	htain de
to smile (vi)	ြပုံးသည်	pjoun: de
to speak (vi, vt)	ပြောသည်	pjo: de
to steal (money, etc.)	ခိုးသည်	khou: de
to stop (for pause, etc.)	ရပ်သည်	ja' te
to stop (please ~ calling me)	ရပ်သည်	ja' te
to study (vt)	သင်ယူလေ့လာသည်	thin ju lei. la de
to swim (vi)	ရေကူးသည်	jei ku: de
to take (vt)	ယူသည်	ju de
to think (vi, vt)	ထင်သည်	htin de
to threaten (vt)	ြခိမ်းြခောက်သည်	chein: gjau' te
to touch (with hands)	ကိုင်သည်	kain de
to translate (vt)	ဘာသာြပန်သည်	ba dha bjan de
to trust (vt)	ယုံကြည်သည်	joun kji de
to try (attempt)	စမ်းကြည့်သည်	san: kji. de
to turn (e.g., ~ left)	ကွေ့သည်	kwei. de
to underestimate (vt)	လျှော့တွက်သည်	sho. dwe' de
to understand (vt)	နားလည်သည်	na: le de
to unite (vt)	ပေါင်းစည်းသည်	paun: ze: de
to wait (vt)	စောင့်သည်	saun. de
to want (wish, desire)	လိုချင်သည်	lou gjin de
to warn (vt)	သတိပေးသည်	dhadi. pei: de
to work (vi)	အလုပ်လုပ်သည်	alou' lou' te
to write (vt)	ရေးသည်	jei: de
to write down	ရေးထားသည်	jei: da: de

TIME. CALENDAR

17. Weekdays

Monday	တနင်္လာ	tanin: la
Tuesday	အင်္ဂါ	in ga
Wednesday	ဗုဒ္ဓဟူး	bou' da. hu:
Thursday	ကြာသပတေး	kja dha ba. dei:
Friday	သောကြာ	thau' kja
Saturday	စနေ	sanei
Sunday	တနင်္ဂနွေ	tanin: ganwei
today (adv)	ယနေ့	ja. nei.
tomorrow (adv)	မနက်ဖြန်	mane' bjan
the day after tomorrow	သဘက်ခါ	dhabe' kha
yesterday (adv)	မနေ့က	ma. nei. ka.
the day before yesterday	တနေ့က	ta. nei. ga.
day	နေ့	nei.
working day	ရုံးဖွင့်ရက်	joun: hpwin je'
public holiday	ပွဲတော်ရက်	pwe: do je'
day off	ရုံးပိတ်ရက်	joun: bei' je'
weekend	ရုံးပိတ်ရက်များ	joun: hpwin je' mja:
all day long	တနေ့လုံး	ta. nei. loun:
the next day (adv)	နောက်နေ့	nau' nei.
two days ago	လွန်ခဲ့သော နှစ်ရက်က	lun ge: de. hni' ja' ka.
the day before	အကြိုနေ့မှာ	akjou nei. hma
daily (adj)	နေ့စဉ်	nei. zin
every day (adv)	နေ့တိုင်း	nei dain:
week	ရက်သတ္တပတ်	je' tha' daba'
last week (adv)	ပြီးခဲ့တဲ့အပတ်က	pji: ge. de. apa' ka.
next week (adv)	လာမယ့်အပတ်မှာ	la. me. apa' hma
weekly (adj)	အပတ်စဉ်	apa' sin
every week (adv)	အပတ်စဉ်	apa' sin
twice a week	တစ်ပတ် နှစ်ကြိမ်	ti' pa' hni' kjein
every Tuesday	အင်္ဂါနေ့တိုင်း	in ga nei. dain:

18. Hours. Day and night

morning	နံနက်ခင်း	nan ne' gin:
in the morning	နံနက်ခင်းမှာ	nan ne' gin: hma
noon, midday	မွန်းတည့်	mun: de.

in the afternoon	နေ့လယ်စာစားချိန်ပြီးနောက်	nei. le za za: gjein bji: nau'
evening	ညနေခင်း	nja. nei gin:
in the evening	ညနေခင်းမှာ	nja. nei gin: hma
night	ည	nja
at night	ညမှာ	nja hma
midnight	သန်းခေါင်ယံ	than: gaun jan
second	စက္ကန့်	se' kan.
minute	မိနစ်	mi. ni'
hour	နာရီ	na ji
half an hour	နာရီဝက်	na ji we'
a quarter-hour	ဆယ့်ငါးမိနစ်	hse. nga: mi. ni'
fifteen minutes	၁၅ မိနစ်	ta' hse. nga: mi ni'
24 hours	နှစ်ဆယ်လေးနာရီ	hni' hse lei: na ji
sunrise	နေထွက်ချိန်	nei dwe' gjein
dawn	အာရုဏ်ဦး	a joun u:
early morning	နံနက်စောစော	nan ne' so: zo:
sunset	နေဝင်ချိန်	nei win gjein
early in the morning	နံနက်အစောပိုင်း	nan ne' aso: bain:
this morning	ယနေ့နံနက်	ja. nei. nan ne'
tomorrow morning	မနက်ဖြန်နံနက်	mane' bjan nan ne'
this afternoon	ယနေ့နေ့လယ်	ja. nei. nei. le
in the afternoon	နေ့လယ်စာစားချိန်ပြီးနောက်	nei. le za za: gjein bji: nau'
tomorrow afternoon	မနက်ဖြန်မွန်းလွဲပိုင်း	mane' bjan mun: lwe: bain:
tonight (this evening)	ယနေ့ညနေ	ja. nei. nja. nei
tomorrow night	မနက်ဖြန်ညနေ	mane' bjan nja. nei
at 3 o'clock sharp	၃ နာရီတွင်	thoun: na ji dwin
about 4 o'clock	၄ နာရီခန့်တွင်	lei: na ji khan dwin
by 12 o'clock	၁၂ နာရီအရောက်	hse. hni' na ji ajau'
in 20 minutes	နောက် မိနစ် ၂၀ မှာ	nau' mi. ni' hni' se hma
in an hour	နောက်တစ်နာရီမှာ	nau' ti' na ji hma
on time (adv)	အချိန်ကိုက်	achein kai'
a quarter to …	မတ်တင်း	ma' tin:
within an hour	တစ်နာရီအတွင်း	ti' na ji atwin:
every 15 minutes	၁၅ မိနစ်တိုင်း	ta' hse. nga: mi ni' htain:
round the clock	၂၄ နာရီလုံး	hna' hse. lei: na ji

19. Months. Seasons

January	ဇန်နဝါရီလ	zan na. wa ji la.
February	ဖေဖော်ဝါရီလ	hpei bo wa ji la
March	မတ်လ	ma' la.
April	ဧပြီလ	ei bji la.

May	မေလ	mei la.
June	ဇွန်လ	zun la.

July	ဇူလိုင်လ	zu lain la.
August	ဩဂုတ်လ	o: gou' la.
September	စက်တင်ဘာလ	sa' htin ba la.
October	အောက်တိုဘာလ	au' tou ba la
November	နိုဝင်ဘာလ	nou win ba la.
December	ဒီဇင်ဘာလ	di zin ba la.

spring	နွေဦးရာသီ	nwei: u: ja dhi
in spring	နွေဦးရာသီမှာ	nwei: u: ja dhi hma
spring (as adj)	နွေဦးရာသီနှင့်ဆိုင်သော	nwei: u: ja dhi hnin. zain de.

summer	နွေရာသီ	nwei: ja dhi
in summer	နွေရာသီမှာ	nwei: ja dhi hma
summer (as adj)	နွေရာသီနှင့်ဆိုင်သော	nwei: ja dhi hnin. zain de.

fall	ဆောင်းဦးရာသီ	hsaun: u: ja dhi
in fall	ဆောင်းဦးရာသီမှာ	hsaun: u: ja dhi hma
fall (as adj)	ဆောင်းဦးရာသီနှင့်ဆိုင်သော	hsaun: u: ja dhi hnin. zain de.

winter	ဆောင်းရာသီ	hsaun: ja dhi
in winter	ဆောင်းရာသီမှာ	hsaun: ja dhi hma
winter (as adj)	ဆောင်းရာသီနှင့်ဆိုင်သော	hsaun: ja dhi hnin. zain de.

month	လ	la.
this month	ဒီလ	di la.
next month	နောက်လ	nau' la
last month	ယခင်လ	jakhin la.

a month ago	ပြီးခဲ့တဲ့တစ်လကျော်	pji: ge. de. di' la. gjo
in a month (a month later)	နောက်တစ်လကျော်	nau' ti' la. gjo
in 2 months (2 months later)	နောက်နှစ်လကျော်	nau' hni' la. gjo
the whole month	တစ်လလုံး	ti' la. loun:
all month long	တစ်လလုံး	ti' la. loun:

monthly (~ magazine)	လစဉ်	la. zin
monthly (adv)	လစဉ်	la. zin
every month	လတိုင်း	la. dain:
twice a month	တစ်လနှစ်ကြိမ်	ti' la. hni' kjein:

year	နှစ်	hni'
this year	ဒီနှစ်မှာ	di hna' hma
next year	နောက်နှစ်မှာ	nau' hni' hnma
last year	ယခင်နှစ်မှာ	jakhin hni' hma

a year ago	ပြီးခဲ့တဲ့တစ်နှစ်ကျော်က	pji: ge. de. di' hni' kjo ga.
in a year	နောက်တစ်နှစ်ကျော်	nau' ti' hni' gjo

in two years	နောက်နှစ်နှစ်ကျော်	nau' hni' hni' gjo
the whole year	တစ်နှစ်လုံး	ti' hni' loun:
all year long	တစ်နှစ်လုံး	ti' hni' loun:
every year	နှစ်တိုင်း	hni' tain:
annual (adj)	နှစ်စဉ်ဖြစ်သော	hni' san bji' te.
annually (adv)	နှစ်စဉ်	hni' san
4 times a year	တစ်နှစ်လေးကြိမ်	ti' hni' lei: gjein
date (e.g., today's ~)	နေ့စွဲ	nei. zwe:
date (e.g., ~ of birth)	ရက်စွဲ	je' swe:
calendar	ပြက္ခဒိန်	pje' gadein
half a year	နှစ်ဝက်	hni' we'
six months	နှစ်ဝက်	hni' we'
season (summer, etc.)	ရာသီ	ja dhi
century	ရာစု	jazu.

TRAVEL. HOTEL

20. Trip. Travel

tourism, travel	ခရီးသွားလုပ်ငန်း	khaji: thwa: lou' ngan:
tourist	ကမ္ဘာလှည့်ခရီးသည်	ga ba hli. kha. ji: de
trip, voyage	ခရီးထွက်ခြင်း	khaji: htwe' chin:
adventure	စွန့်စားမှု	sun. za: hmu.
trip, journey	ခရီး	khaji:
vacation	ခွင့်ရက်	khwin. je'
to be on vacation	အခွင့်ယူသည်	akhwin. ju de
rest	အနားယူခြင်း	ana: ju gjin:
train	ရထား	jatha:
by train	ရထားနဲ့	jatha: ne.
airplane	လေယာဉ်	lei jan
by airplane	လေယာဉ်နဲ့	lei jan ne.
by car	ကားနဲ့	ka: ne.
by ship	သင်္ဘောနဲ့	thin: bo: ne.
luggage	ဝန်စည်စလည်	wun zi za. li
suitcase	သားရေသေတ္တာ	tha: jei dhi' ta
luggage cart	ပစ္စည်းတင်ရန်တွန်းလှည်း	pji' si: din jan dun: hle:
passport	နိုင်ငံကူးလက်မှတ်	nain ngan gu: le' hma'
visa	ဗီဇာ	bi za
ticket	လက်မှတ်	le' hma'
air ticket	လေယာဉ်လက်မှတ်	lei jan le' hma'
guidebook	လမ်းညွှန်စာအုပ်	lan: hnjun za ou'
map (tourist ~)	မြေပုံ	mjei boun
area (rural ~)	ဒေသ	dei dha.
place, site	နေရာ	nei ja
exotica (n)	အထူးအဆန်းပစ္စည်း	a htu: a hsan: bji' si:
exotic (adj)	အထူးအဆန်းဖြစ်သော	a htu: a hsan: hpja' te.
amazing (adj)	အံ့သြစရာကောင်းသော	an. o: sa ja kaun de.
group	အုပ်စု	ou' zu.
excursion, sightseeing tour	လေ့လာရေးခရီး	lei. la jei: gaji:
guide (person)	လမ်းညွှန်	lan: hnjun

21. Hotel

hotel	ဟိုတယ်	hou te
motel	မိုတယ်	mou te
three-star (~ hotel)	ကြယ် ၃ ပွင့်အဆင့်	kje thoun: pwin. ahsin.
five-star	ကြယ် ၅ ပွင့်အဆင့်	kje nga: pwin. ahsin.
to stay (in a hotel, etc.)	တည်းခိုသည်	te: khou de
room	အခန်း	akhan:
single room	တစ်ယောက်ခန်း	ti' jau' khan:
double room	နှစ်ယောက်ခန်း	hni' jau' khan:
to book a room	ကြိုတင်မှာယူသည်	kjou tin hma ju de
half board	ကြိုတင်တွစ်ဝက်ငွေချေခြင်း	kjou tin di' we' ngwe gjei gjin:
full board	ငွေအပြည့်ကြိုတင်ပေးခြေခြင်း	ngwei apjei. kjou din bei: chei chin:
with bath	ရေချိုးခန်းနှင့်	jei gjou gan: hnin.
with shower	ရေပန်းနှင့်	jei ban: hnin.
satellite television	ဂြိုလ်တုရုပ်မြင်သံကြား	gjou' htu. jou' mjin dhan gja:
air-conditioner	လေအေးပေးစက်	lei ei: bei: ze'
towel	တဘက်	tabe'
key	သော့	tho.
administrator	အုပ်ချုပ်ရေးမှူး	ou' chu' jei: hmu:
chambermaid	သန့်ရှင်းရေးဝန်ထမ်း	than. shin: jei: wun dan:
porter, bellboy	အထမ်းသမား	a htan: dha. ma:
doorman	တံခါးဝမှ စောင့်ကြို	daga: wa. hma. e. kjou
restaurant	စားသောက်ဆိုင်	sa: thau' hsain
pub, bar	ဘား	ba:
breakfast	နံနက်စာ	nan ne' za
dinner	ညစာ	nja. za
buffet	ဘူဖေး	bu hpei:
lobby	နားနေရောင်ခန်း	hna jaun gan:
elevator	ဓာတ်လှေကား	da' hlei ga:
DO NOT DISTURB	မနှောင့်ယှက်ရ	ma. hnaun hje' ja.
NO SMOKING	ဆေးလိပ်မသောက်ရ	hsei: lei' ma. dhau' ja.

22. Sightseeing

monument	ရုပ်တု	jou' tu.
fortress	ခံတပ်ကြီး	khwan da' kji:
palace	နန်းတော်	nan do

castle	ရဲတိုက်	je: dai'
tower	မျှော်စင်	hmjo zin
mausoleum	ဂူဗိမာန်	gu bi. man

architecture	ဗိသုကာပညာ	bi. thu. ka pjin nja
medieval (adj)	အလယ်ခေတ်နှင့်ဆိုင်သော	ale khei' hnin. zain de.
ancient (adj)	ရှေးကျသော	shei: gja. de
national (adj)	အမျိုးသားနှင့်ဆိုင်သော	amjou: dha: hnin. zain de.
famous (monument, etc.)	နာမည်ကြီးသော	na me gji: de.

tourist	ကမ္ဘာလှည့်ခရီးသည်	ga ba hli. kha. ji: de
guide (person)	လမ်းညွှန်	lan: hnjun
excursion, sightseeing tour	လေ့လာရေးခရီး	lei: la jei: gaji:
to show (vt)	ပြသည်	pja. de
to tell (vt)	ပြောပြသည်	pjo: bja. de

to find (vt)	ရှာတွေ့သည်	sha dwei. de
to get lost (lose one's way)	ပျောက်သည်	pjau' te
map (e.g., subway ~)	မြေပုံ	mjei boun
map (e.g., city ~)	မြေပုံ	mjei boun

souvenir, gift	အမှတ်တရလက်ဆောင်ပစ္စည်း	ahma' ta ra le' hsaun pji' si:
gift shop	လက်ဆောင်ပစ္စည်းဆိုင်	le' hsaun pji' si: zain
to take pictures	ဓာတ်ပုံရိုက်သည်	da' poun jai' te
to have one's picture taken	ဓာတ်ပုံရိုက်သည်	da' poun jai' te

TRANSPORTATION

23. Airport

airport	လေဆိပ်	lei zi'
airplane	လေယာဉ်	lei jan
airline	လေကြောင်း	lei gjaun:
air traffic controller	လေကြောင်းထိန်း	lei kjaun: din:
departure	ထွက်ခွာရာ	htwe' khwa ja
arrival	ဆိုက်ရောက်ရာ	hseu' jau' ja
to arrive (by plane)	ဆိုက်ရောက်သည်	hsai' jau' te
departure time	ထွက်ခွာချိန်	htwe' khwa gjein
arrival time	ဆိုက်ရောက်ချိန်	hseu' jau' chein
to be delayed	နောက်ကျသည်	nau' kja. de
flight delay	လေယာဉ်နောက်ကျခြင်း	lei jan nau' kja. chin:
information board	လေယာဉ်ခရီးစဉ်ပြဘုတ်	lei jan ga. ji: zi bja. bou'
information	သတင်းအချက်အလက်	dhadin: akje' ale'
to announce (vt)	ကြေငြာသည်	kjei nja de
flight (e.g., next ~)	ပျံသန်းမှု	pjan dan: hmu.
customs	အကောက်ဆိပ်	akau' hsein
customs officer	အကောက်ခွန်အရာရှိ	akau' khun aja shi.
customs declaration	အကောက်ခွန်ကြေငြာချက်	akau' khun gjei nja gje'
to fill out (vt)	လျှောက်လွှာဖြည့်သည်	shau' hlwa bji. de
to fill out the declaration	သည့်ယူပစ္စည်းစာရင်း	the ju pji' si: zajin:
	ကြေညာသည်	kjei nja de
passport control	ပတ်စ်ပို့ထိန်းချုပ်မှု	pa's pou. htein: gju' hmu.
luggage	ဝန်စည်စလည်	wun zi za. li
hand luggage	လက်ဆွဲပစ္စည်း	le' swe: pji' si:
luggage cart	ပစ္စည်းတင်သည့်လှည်း	pji' si: din dhe. hle:
landing	ဆင်းသက်ခြင်း	hsin: dha' chin:
landing strip	အဆင်းလမ်း	ahsin: lan:
to land (vi)	ဆင်းသက်သည်	hsin: dha' te
airstair (passenger stair)	လေယာဉ်လှေကား	lei jan hlei ka:
check-in	စာရင်းသွင်းခြင်း	sajin: dhwin: gjin:
check-in counter	စာရင်းသွင်းကောင်တာ	sajin: gaun da
to check-in (vi)	စာရင်းသွင်းသည်	sajin: dhwin: de
boarding pass	လေယာဉ်ပေါ်တက်	lei jan bo de'
	ခွင့်လက်မှတ်	khwin. le' hma'

departure gate	လေယာဉ်ထွက်ခွာရာဂိတ်	lei jan dwe' khwa ja gei'
transit	အကူးအပြောင်း	aku: apjaun:
to wait (vt)	စောင့်သည်	saun. de
departure lounge	ထွက်ခွာရာခန်းမ	htwe' kha ja gan: ma.
to see off	လိုက်ပို့သည်	lai' bou. de
to say goodbye	နှုတ်ဆက်သည်	hnou' hsei' te

24. Airplane

airplane	လေယာဉ်	lei jan
air ticket	လေယာဉ်လက်မှတ်	lei jan le' hma'
airline	လေကြောင်း	lei gjaun:
airport	လေဆိပ်	lei zi'
supersonic (adj)	အသံထက်မြန်သော	athan de' mjan de.
captain	လေယာဉ်မှူး	lei jan hmu:
crew	လေယာဉ်အမှုထမ်းအဖွဲ့	lei jan ahmu. dan: ahpwe.
pilot	လေယာဉ်မောင်းသူ	lei jan maun dhu
flight attendant (fem.)	လေယာဉ်မယ်	lei jan me
navigator	လေကြောင်းပြ	lei gjaun: bja.
wings	လေယာဉ်တောင်ပံ	lei jan daun ban
tail	လေယာဉ်အမြီး	lei jan amji:
cockpit	လေယာဉ်မောင်းအခန်း	lei jan maun akhan:
engine	အင်ဂျင်	in gjin
undercarriage (landing gear)	အောက်ခံဘောင်	au' khan baun
turbine	တာဘိုင်	ta bain
propeller	ပန်ကာ	pan ga
black box	ဘလက်ဘောက်	ba. le' bo'
yoke (control column)	ပဲ့ကိုင်ဘီး	pe. gain bi:
fuel	လောင်စာ	laun za
safety card	အရေးပေါ်လုံခြုံရေး ညွှန်ကြားစာ	ajei: po' choun loun jei: hnjun gja: za
oxygen mask	အောက်ဆီဂျင်မျက်နှာဖုံး	au' hsi gjin mje' hna hpoun:
uniform	ယူနီဖောင်း	ju ni hpaun:
life vest	အသက်ကယ်အင်္ကျီ	athe' kai in: gji
parachute	လေထီး	lei di:
takeoff	ထွက်ခွါခြင်း	htwe' khwa gjin:
to take off (vi)	ပျံတက်သည်	pjan de' te
runway	လေယာဉ်ပြေးလမ်း	lei jan bei: lan:
visibility	မြင်ကွင်း	mjin gwin:
flight (act of flying)	ပျံသန်းခြင်း	pjan dan: gjin:
altitude	အမြင့်	amjin.
air pocket	လေမငြိမ်အရပ်	lei ma ngjin aja'

seat	ထိုင်ခုံ	htain goun
headphones	နားကြပ်	na: kja'
folding tray (tray table)	ခေါက်စားပွဲ	khau' sa: bwe:
airplane window	လေယာဉ်ပြတင်းပေါက်	lei jan bja. din: bau'
aisle	မင်းလမ်း	min: lan:

25. Train

train	ရထား	jatha:
commuter train	လျုပ်စစ်ဓာတ်အားသုံးရထား	hlja' si' da' a: dhou: ja da:
express train	အမြန်ရထား	aman ja. hta:
diesel locomotive	ဒီဇယ်ရထား	di ze ja da:
steam locomotive	ရေနွေးငွေ့စက်ခေါင်း	jei nwei: ngwei. ze' khaun:
passenger car	အတွဲ	atwe:
dining car	စားသောက်တွဲ	sa: thau' thwe:
rails	ရထားသံလမ်း	jatha dhan lan:
railroad	ရထားလမ်း	jatha: lan:
railway tie	ဇလီဖားတုံး	zali ba: doun
platform (railway ~)	စကြန်	sin gjan
track (~ 1, 2, etc.)	ရထားစကြန်	jatha zin gjan
semaphore	မီးပွိုင့်	mi: bwain.
station	ဘူတာရုံ	bu da joun
engineer (train driver)	ရထားမောင်းသူ	jatha: maun: dhu
porter (of luggage)	အထမ်းသမား	a htan: dha. ma:
car attendant	အစောင့်	asaun.
passenger	ခရီးသည်	khaji: de
conductor (ticket inspector)	လက်မှတ်စစ်ဆေးသူ	le' hma' ti' hsei: dhu:
corridor (in train)	ကော်ရစ်တာ	ko ji' ta
emergency brake	အရေးပေါ် ဘရိတ်	ajei: po' ba ji'
compartment	အခန်း	akhan:
berth	အိပ်စင်	ei' zin
upper berth	အပေါ်ထပ်အိပ်စင်	apo htap ei' sin
lower berth	အောက်ထပ်အိပ်စင်	au' hta' ei' sin
bed linen, bedding	အိပ်ရာခင်း	ei' ja khin:
ticket	လက်မှတ်	le' hma'
schedule	အချိန်ဇယား	achein zaja:
information display	အချက်အလက်ပြနေရာ	ache ale' pja. nei ja
to leave, to depart	ထွက်ခွါသည်	htwe' khwa de
departure (of train)	အထွက်	a htwe'
to arrive (ab. train)	ဆိုက်ရောက်သည်	hseu' jau' de
arrival	ဆိုက်ရောက်ရာ	hseu' jau' ja

to arrive by train	ဦးရထားဖြင့်ရောက်ရှိသည်	mi: ja. da: bjin. jau' shi. de
to get on the train	ဦးရထားစီးသည်	mi: ja. da: zi: de
to get off the train	ဦးရထားမှဆင်းသည်	mi: ja. da: hma. zin: de

| train wreck | ရထားတိုက်ခြင်း | jatha: dai' chin: |
| to derail (vi) | ရထားလမ်းချော်သည် | jatha: lan: gjo de |

steam locomotive	ရေနွေးငွေ့စက်ခေါင်း	jei nwei: ngwei. ze' khaun:
stoker, fireman	ဦးထိုးသမား	mi: dou: dhama:
firebox	ဦးဖို	mi: bou
coal	ကျောက်မီးသွေး	kjau' mi dhwei:

26. Ship

| ship | သင်္ဘော | thin: bo: |
| vessel | ရေယာဉ် | jei jan |

steamship	ဦးသင်္ဘော	mi: dha. bo:
riverboat	အပျော်စီးမော်တော်ဘုတ်ငယ်	apjo zi: mo do bou' nge
cruise ship	ပင်လယ်အပျော်စီးသင်္ဘော	pin le apjo zi: dhin: bo:
cruiser	လေယာဉ်တင်သင်္ဘော	lei jan din

yacht	အပျော်စီးရွက်လှေ	apjo zi: jwe' hlei
tugboat	ဆွဲသင်္ဘော	hswe: thin: bo:
barge	ဖောင်	hpaun
ferry	ကူးတို့သင်္ဘော	gadou. thin: bo:

| sailing ship | ရွက်သင်္ဘော | jwe' thin: bo: |
| brigantine | ရွက်လှေ | jwe' hlei |

| ice breaker | ရေခဲပြင်ခွဲသင်္ဘော | jei ge: bjin gwe: dhin: bo: |
| submarine | ရေငုပ်သင်္ဘော | jei ngou' thin: bo: |

boat (flat-bottomed ~)	လှေ	hlei
dinghy (lifeboat)	ရော်ဘာလှေ	jo ba hlei
lifeboat	အသက်ကယ်လှေ	athe' kai hlei
motorboat	မော်တော်ဘုတ်	mo to bou'

captain	ရေယာဉ်မှူး	jei jan hmu:
seaman	သင်္ဘောသား	thin: bo: dha:
sailor	သင်္ဘောသား	thin: bo: dha:
crew	သင်္ဘောအမှုထမ်း အဖွဲ့	thin: bo: ahmu. htan: ahpwe.

boatswain	ရေတပ်အရာရှိငယ်	jei da' aja shi. nge
ship's boy	သင်္ဘောသားကောလေး	thin: bo: dha: galei:
cook	ထမင်းချက်	htamin: gje'
ship's doctor	သင်္ဘောဆရာဝန်	thin: bo: zaja wun
deck	သင်္ဘောကုန်းပတ်	thin: bo: koun: ba'
mast	ရွက်တိုင်	jwe' tai'

sail	ရွက်	jwe'
hold	ဝမ်းတွင်း	wan: twin:
bow (prow)	ဦးစွန်း	u: zun:
stern	ပဲ့ပိုင်း	pe. bain:
oar	လှော်တက်	hlo de'
screw propeller	သင်္ဘောပန်ကာ	thin: bo: ban ga
cabin	သင်္ဘောပေါ်မှအခန်း	thin: bo: bo hma. aksan:
wardroom	အရာရှိများရိပ်သာ	aja shi. mja: jin dha
engine room	စက်ခန်း	se' khan:
bridge	ကွပ်ကဲခန်း	ku' ke: khan:
radio room	ရေဒီယိုခန်း	rei di jou gan:
wave (radio)	လှိုင်း	hlain:
logbook	မှတ်တမ်းစာအုပ်	hma' tan: za ou'
spyglass	အဝေးကြည့်မှန်ပြောင်း	awei: gji. hman bjaun:
bell	ခေါင်းလောင်း	gaun: laun:
flag	အလံ	alan
hawser (mooring ~)	သင်္ဘောသုံးလွန်ကြိုး	thin: bo: dhaun: lun gjou:
knot (bowline, etc.)	ကြိုးထုံး	kjou: htoun:
deckrails	လက်ရန်း	le' jan
gangway	သင်္ဘောကုန်းပေါင်	thin: bo: koun: baun
anchor	ကျောက်ဆူး	kjau' hsu:
to weigh anchor	ကျောက်ဆူးနုတ်သည်	kjau' hsu: nou' te
to drop anchor	ကျောက်ချသည်	kjau' cha. de
anchor chain	ကျောက်ဆူးကြိုး	kjau' hsu: kjou:
port (harbor)	ဆိပ်ကမ်း	hsi' kan:
quay, wharf	သင်္ဘောဆိပ်	thin: bo: zei'
to berth (moor)	ဆိုက်ကပ်သည်	hseu' ka' de
to cast off	စွန့်ပစ်သည်	sun. bi' de
trip, voyage	ခရီးထွက်ခြင်း	khaji: htwe' chin:
cruise (sea trip)	အပျော်ခရီး	apjo gaji:
course (route)	ဦးတည်ရာ	u: ti ja
route (itinerary)	လမ်းကြောင်း	lan: gjaun:
fairway (safe water channel)	သင်္ဘောရေကြောင်း	thin: bo: jei gjaun:
shallows	ရေတိမ်ပိုင်း	jei dein bain:
to run aground	ကမ်းကပ်သည်	kan ka' te
storm	မုန်တိုင်း	moun dain:
signal	အချက်ပြ	ache' pja.
to sink (vi)	နစ်မြုပ်သည်	ni' mjou' te
Man overboard!	လူရေထဲကျ	lu jei de: gja
SOS (distress signal)	အက်စ်အိုအက်စ်	e's o e's
ring buoy	အသက်ကယ်ဘော	athe' kai bo

CITY

bus	ဘတ်စ်ကား	ba's ka:
streetcar	ဓာတ်ရထား	da' ja hta:
trolley bus	ဓာတ်ကား	da' ka:
route (of bus, etc.)	လမ်းကြောင်း	lan: gjaun:
number (e.g., bus ~)	ကားနံပါတ်	ka: nan ba'
to go by ...	ယဉ်စီးသည်	jin zi: de
to get on (~ the bus)	ထိုင်သည်	htain de
to get off ...	ကားပေါ်မှဆင်းသည်	ka: bo hma. zin: de
stop (e.g., bus ~)	မှတ်တိုင်	hma' tain
next stop	နောက်မှတ်တိုင်	nau' hma' tain
terminus	အဆုံးမှတ်တိုင်	ahsoun: hma' tain
schedule	အချိန်ဇယား	achein zaja:
to wait (vt)	စောင့်သည်	saun. de
ticket	လက်မှတ်	le' hma'
fare	ယဉ်စီးခ	jin zi: ga.
cashier (ticket seller)	ငွေကိုင်	ngwei gain
ticket inspection	လက်မှတ်စစ်ဆေးခြင်း	le' hma' ti' hsei: chin
ticket inspector	လက်မှတ်စစ်ဆေးသူ	le' hma' ti' hsei: dhu:
to be late (for ...)	နောက်ကျသည်	nau' kja. de
to miss (~ the train, etc.)	ကားနောက်ကျသည်	ka: nau' kja de
to be in a hurry	အမြန်လုပ်သည်	aman lou' de
taxi, cab	တက္ကစီ	te' kasi
taxi driver	တက္ကစီမောင်းသူ	te' kasi maun: dhu
by taxi	တက္ကစီဖြင့်	te' kasi hpjin.
taxi stand	တက္ကစီရပ်ဝင်	te' kasi zu. ja'
to call a taxi	တက္ကစီခေါ်သည်	te' kasi go de
to take a taxi	တက္ကစီငှားသည်	te' kasi hnga: de
traffic	ယဉ်အသွားအလာ	jin athwa: ala
traffic jam	ယဉ်ကြောပိတ်ဆို့.မှု	jin gjo: bei' hsou. hmu.
rush hour	အလုပ်ဆင်းချိန်	alou' hsin: gjain
to park (vi)	ယဉ်ရပ်နားရန်နေရာယူသည်	jin ja' na: jan nei ja ju de
to park (vt)	ကားအားပါကင်ထိုးသည်	ka: a: pa kin dou: de
parking lot	ပါကင်	pa gin
subway	မြေအောက်ဥမင်လမ်း	mjei au' u. min lan:
station	ဘူတာရုံ	bu da joun

to take the subway	မြေအောက်ရထား ဖြင့်သွားသည်	mjei au' ja. da: bjin. dhwa: de
train	ရထား	jatha:
train station	ရထားဘူတာရုံ	jatha: buda joun

28. City. Life in the city

city, town	မြို့	mjou.
capital city	မြို့တော်	mjou. do
village	ရွာ	jwa

city map	မြို့လမ်းညွှန်မြေပုံ	mjou. lan hnjun mjei boun
downtown	မြို့လယ်ခေါင်	mjou. le gaun
suburb	ဆင်ခြေဖုံးအရပ်	hsin gjei aja'
suburban (adj)	ဆင်ခြေဖုံး အရပ်ဖြစ်သော	hsin gjei hpoun aja' hpa' te.

outskirts	မြို့စွန်	mjou. zun
environs (suburbs)	ပတ်ဝန်းကျင်	pa' wun: gjin:
city block	စည်ကားရာမြို့လယ်နေရာ	si: ga: ja mjou. le nei ja
residential block (area)	လူနေရပ်ကွက်	lu nei ja' kwe'

traffic	ယာဉ်အသွားအလာ	jin athwa: ala
traffic lights	မီးပွိုင့်	mi: bwain.
public transportation	ပြည်သူ့ပိုင်ခရီးသွား ့စီးဆောင်ရေး	pji dhu bain gaji: dhwa: bou. zaun jei:
intersection	လမ်းဆုံ	lan: zoun

crosswalk	လူကူးမျဉ်းကြား	lu gu: mji: gja:
pedestrian underpass	မြေအောက်လမ်းကူး	mjei au' lan: gu:
to cross (~ the street)	လမ်းကူးသည်	lan: gu: de
pedestrian	လမ်းသွားလမ်းလာ	lan: dhwa: lan: la
sidewalk	လူသွားလမ်း	lu dhwa: lan:

bridge	တံတား	dada:
embankment (river walk)	ကမ်းနားတမံ	kan: na: da. man
fountain	ရေပန်း	jei ban:

allée (garden walkway)	ရိပ်သာလမ်း	jei' tha lan:
park	ပန်းခြံ	pan: gjan
boulevard	လမ်းဝယ်	lan: ge
square	ရင်ပြင်	jin bjin
avenue (wide street)	လမ်းမကြီး	lan: mi. gji:
street	လမ်း	lan:
side street	လမ်းသွယ်	lan: dhwe
dead end	လမ်းဆုံး	lan: zoun:

house	အိမ်	ein
building	အဆောက်အဦ	ahsau' au
skyscraper	မိုးမျှော်တိုက်	mou: hmjo tou'

facade	အိမ်ရှေ့နံရံ	ein shei. nan jan
roof	အမိုး	amou:
window	ပြတင်းပေါက်	badin: pau'
arch	မုဒ်ဝ	mou' wa.
column	တိုင်	tain
corner	ထောင့်	htaun.

store window	ဆိုင်ရှေ့ပစ္စည်း အခင်းအကျင်း	hseun shei. bji' si: akhin: akjin:
signboard (store sign, etc.)	ဆိုင်းဘုတ်	hsain: bou'
poster (e.g., playbill)	ပိုစတာ	pou sata
advertising poster	ကြော်ငြာပိုစတာ	kjo nja bou sata
billboard	ကြော်ငြာဆိုင်းဘုတ်	kjo nja zain: bou'

garbage, trash	အမှိုက်	ahmai'
trash can (public ~)	အမှိုက်ပုံး	ahmai' poun:
to litter (vi)	လွှင့်ပစ်သည်	hlwin. bi' te
garbage dump	အမှိုက်ပုံ	ahmai' poun

phone booth	တယ်လီဖုန်းဆက်ရန်နေရာ	te li hpoun: ze' jan nei ja
lamppost	လမ်းမီး	lan: mi:
bench (park ~)	ခုံတန်းရှည်	khoun dan: shei

police officer	ရဲ	je:
police	ရဲ	je:
beggar	သူတောင်းစား	thu daun: za:
homeless (n)	အိမ်ယာမဲ့	ein ja me.

29. Urban institutions

store	ဆိုင်	hsain
drugstore, pharmacy	ဆေးဆိုင်	hsei: zain
eyeglass store	မျက်မှန်ဆိုင်	mje' hman zain
shopping mall	ဈေးဝင်ဝင်တာ	zei: wun zin da
supermarket	ကုန်တိုက်ကြီး	koun dou' kji:

bakery	မုန့်တိုက်	moun. dai'
baker	ပေါင်မုန့်ဖုတ်သူ	paun moun. bou' dhu
pastry shop	မုန့်ဆိုင်	moun. zain
grocery store	ကုန်စုံဆိုင်	koun zoun zain
butcher shop	အသားဆိုင်	atha: ain

produce store	ဟင်းသီးဟင်းရွက်ဆိုင်	hin: dhi: hin: jwe' hsain
market	ဈေး	zei:

coffee house	ကော်ဖီဆိုင်	ko hpi zain
restaurant	စားသောက်ဆိုင်	sa: thau' hsain
pub, bar	ဘီယာဆိုင်	bi ja zain:
pizzeria	ဝိဇ္ဇာမုန့်ဆိုင်	pi za moun. zain
hair salon	ဆံပင်ညှပ်ဆိုင်	zain hnja' hsain

post office	စာတိုက်	sa dai'
dry cleaners	အဝတ်အခြောက်လျှော် လုပ်ငန်း	awu' achou' hlo: lou' ngan:
photo studio	ဓာတ်ပုံရိုက်ခန်း	da' poun jai' khan:
shoe store	ဖိနပ်ဆိုင်	hpana' sain
bookstore	စာအုပ်ဆိုင်	sa ou' hsain
sporting goods store	အားကစားပစ္စည်းဆိုင်	a: gaza: pji' si: zain
clothes repair shop	စက်ပြင်ဆိုင်	se' pjin zain
formal wear rental	ဝတ်စုံအငှါးဆိုင်	wa' zoun ahnga: zain
video rental store	အခွေငှါးဆိုင်	akhwei hnga: zain:
circus	ဆပ်ကပ်	hsa' ka'
zoo	တိရစ္ဆာန်ဥယျာဉ်	tharei' hsan u. jin
movie theater	ရုပ်ရှင်ရုံ	jou' shin joun
museum	ပြတိုက်	pja. dai'
library	စာကြည့်တိုက်	sa gji. dai'
theater	ကဇာတ်ရုံ	ka. za' joun
opera (opera house)	အော်ပရာဇာတ်ရုံ	o pa ra za' joun
nightclub	နိုက်ကလပ်	nai' ka. la'
casino	လောင်းကစားရုံ	laun: gaza: joun
mosque	ဗလီ	bali
synagogue	ရှုဟူဒီဘုရား ရှိခိုးကျောင်း	ja. hu di bu. ja: shi. gou: gjaun:
cathedral	ဘုရားရှိခိုးကျောင်းတော်	hpaja: gjaun: do:
temple	ဘုရားကျောင်း	hpaja: gjaun:
church	ဘုရားကျောင်း	hpaja: gjaun:
college	တက္ကသိုလ်	te' kathou
university	တက္ကသိုလ်	te' kathou
school	စာသင်ကျောင်း	sa dhin gjaun:
prefecture	စီရင်စုနယ်	si jin zu. ne
city hall	မြို့တော်ခန်းမ	mjou. do gan: ma.
hotel	ဟိုတယ်	hou te
bank	ဘဏ်	ban
embassy	သံရုံး	than joun:
travel agency	ခရီးသွားလုပ်ငန်း	khaji: thwa: lou' ngan:
information office	သတင်းအချက်အလက်ဌာန	dhadin: akje' ale' hta. na.
currency exchange	ငွေလဲရန်နေရာ	ngwei le: jan nei ja
subway	မြေအောက်ဥမင်လမ်း	mjei au' u. min lan:
hospital	ဆေးရုံ	hsei: joun
gas station	ဆီဆိုင်	hsi: zain
parking lot	ကားပါကင်	ka: pa kin

30. Signs

signboard (store sign, etc.)	ဆိုင်းဘုတ်	hsain: bou'
notice (door sign, etc.)	သတိပေးစာ	dhadi. pei: za
poster	ပိုစတာ	pou sata
direction sign	လမ်းညွှန်	lan: hnjun
arrow (sign)	လမ်းညွှန်မြား	lan: hnjun hmja:
caution	သတိပေးခြင်း	dhadi. pei: gjin:
warning sign	သတိပေးချက်	dhadi. pei: gje'
to warn (vt)	သတိပေးသည်	dhadi. pei: de
rest day (weekly ~)	ရုံးပိတ်ရက်	joun: bei' je'
timetable (schedule)	အချိန်ဇယား	achein zaja:
opening hours	ဖွင့်ချိန်	hpwin. gjin
WELCOME!	ကြိုဆိုပါသည်	kjou hsou ba de
ENTRANCE	ဝင်ပေါက်	win bau'
EXIT	ထွက်ပေါက်	htwe' pau'
PUSH	တွန်းသည်	tun: de
PULL	ဆွဲသည်	hswe: de
OPEN	ဖွင့်သည်	hpwin. de
CLOSED	ပိတ်သည်	pei' te
WOMEN	အမျိုးသမီးသုံး	amjou: dhami: dhoun:
MEN	အမျိုးသားသုံး	amjou: dha: dhoun:
DISCOUNTS	လျှော့ဈေး	sho. zei:
SALE	လျှော့ဈေး	sho. zei:
NEW!	အသစ်	athi'
FREE	အခမဲ့	akha me.
ATTENTION!	သတိ	thadi.
NO VACANCIES	အလွတ်မရှိ	alu' ma shi.
RESERVED	ကြိုတင်မှာယူထားပြီး	kjou tin hma ju da: bji:
ADMINISTRATION	စီမံအုပ်ချုပ်ခြင်း	si man ou' chou' chin:
STAFF ONLY	အမှုထမ်းအတွက်အသာ	ahmu. htan: atwe' atha
BEWARE OF THE DOG!	ခွေးကိုက်တတ်သည်	khwei: kai' ta' te
NO SMOKING	ဆေးလိပ်မသောက်ရ	hsei: lei' ma. dhau' ja.
DO NOT TOUCH!	မထိရ	ma. di. ja.
DANGEROUS	အန္တရာယ်ရှိသည်	an dare shi. de.
DANGER	အန္တရာယ်	an dare
HIGH VOLTAGE	ဗို့အားပြင်း	bou. a: bjin:
NO SWIMMING!	ရေမကူးရ	jei ma. gu: ja.
OUT OF ORDER	ပျက်နေသည်	pje' nei de
FLAMMABLE	မီးလောင်တတ်သည်	mi: laun da' te
FORBIDDEN	တားမြစ်သည်	ta: mji' te

NO TRESPASSING!	မကျူးကျော်ရ	ma. gju: gjo ja
WET PAINT	ဆေးမခြောက်သေး	hsei: ma. gjau' dhei:

31. Shopping

to buy (purchase)	ဝယ်သည်	we de
purchase	ဝယ်စရာ	we zaja
to go shopping	ဈေးဝယ်ထွက်ခြင်း	zei: we htwe' chin:
shopping	ရှော့ပင်း	sho. bin:
to be open (ab. store)	ဆိုင်ဖွင့်သည်	hsain bwin. de
to be closed	ဆိုင်ပိတ်သည်	hseun bi' te
footwear, shoes	ဖိနပ်	hpana'
clothes, clothing	အဝတ်အစား	awu' aza:
cosmetics	အလှကုန်ပစ္စည်း	ahla. koun pji' si:
food products	စားသောက်ကုန်	sa: thau' koun
gift, present	လက်ဆောင်	le' hsaun
salesman	ရောင်းသူ	jaun: dhu
saleswoman	ရောင်းသူ	jaun: dhu
check out, cash desk	ငွေရှင်းရန်နေရာ	ngwei shin: jan nei ja
mirror	မှန်	hman
counter (store ~)	ကောင်တာ	kaun da
fitting room	အဝတ်လဲခန်း	awu' le: gan:
to try on	တိုင်းကြည့်သည်	tain: dhi. de
to fit (ab. dress, etc.)	သင့်တော်သည်	thin. do de
to like (I like …)	ကြိုက်သည်	kjai' de
price	ဈေးနှုန်း	zei: hnan:
price tag	ဈေးနှုန်းကတ်ပြား	zei: hnan: ka' pja:
to cost (vt)	ကုန်ကျသည်	koun mja. de
How much?	ဘယ်လောက်လဲ	be lau' le:
discount	လျှော့ဈေး	sho. zei:
inexpensive (adj)	ဈေးမကြီးသော	zei: ma. kji: de.
cheap (adj)	ဈေးပေါသော	zei: po: de.
expensive (adj)	ဈေးကြီးသော	zei: kji: de.
It's expensive	ဒါဈေးကြီးတယ်	da zei: gji: de
rental (n)	ငှားရမ်းခြင်း	hna: jan: chin:
to rent (~ a tuxedo)	ငှားရမ်းသည်	hna: jan: de
credit (trade credit)	အကြွေးစနစ်	akjwei: sani'
on credit (adv)	အကြွေးစနစ်ဖြင့်	akjwei: sa ni' hpjin.

CLOTHING & ACCESSORIES

32. Outerwear. Coats

clothes	အဝတ်အစား	awu' aza:
outerwear	အပေါ်ဝတ်အကျို	apo we' in: gji
winter clothing	ဆောင်းတွင်းဝတ်အဝတ်အစား	hsaun: dwin: wu' awu' asa:
coat (overcoat)	ကုတ်အကျိုရှည်	kou' akji shi
fur coat	သားမွေးအနွေးထည်	tha: mwei: anwei: de
fur jacket	အမွေးပွအပေါ်အကျို	ahmwei pwa po akji.
down coat	ငှက်မွေးကုတ်အကျို	hnge' hmwei: kou' akji.
jacket (e.g., leather ~)	အပေါ်အကျို	apo akji.
raincoat (trenchcoat, etc.)	မိုးကာအကျို	mou: ga akji
waterproof (adj)	ရေလုံသော	jei loun de.

33. Men's & women's clothing

shirt (button shirt)	ရှပ်အကျို	sha' in gji
pants	ဘောင်းဘီ	baun: bi
jeans	ဂျင်းဘောင်းဘီ	gjin: bain: bi
suit jacket	အပေါ်အကျို	apo akji.
suit	အနောက်တိုင်းဝတ်စုံ	anau' tain: wu' saun
dress (frock)	ဂါဝန်	ga wun
skirt	စကတ်	saka'
blouse	ဘလောက်စ်အကျို	ba. lau' s in: gji
knitted jacket (cardigan, etc.)	ကြယ်သီးပါသော အနွေးထည်	kje dhi: ba de. anwei: dhe
jacket (of woman's suit)	အပေါ်ဖုံးအကျို	apo hpoun akji.
T-shirt	တီရှပ်	ti shi'
shorts (short trousers)	ဘောင်းဘီတို	baun: bi dou
tracksuit	အားကစားဝတ်စုံ	a: gaza: wu' soun
bathrobe	ရေချိုးခန်းဝတ်စုံ	jei gjou: gan: wu' soun
pajamas	ညအိပ်ဝတ်စုံ	nja a' wu' soun
sweater	ဆွယ်တာ	hswe da
pullover	ဆွယ်တာ	hswe da
vest	ဝစ်ကုတ်	wi' kou'
tailcoat	တေးလ်ကုတ်အကျို	tei: l kou' in: gji
tuxedo	ညစာစားပွဲဝတ်စုံ	nja. za za: bwe: wu' soun

uniform	တူညီဝတ်စုံ	tu nji wa' soun
workwear	အလုပ်ဝင် ဝတ်စုံ	alou' win wu' zoun
overalls	စက်ရှိဝတ်စုံ	se' joun wu' soun
coat (e.g., doctor's smock)	ဂျူတိကုတ်	gju di gou'

34. Clothing. Underwear

underwear	အတွင်းခံ	atwin: gan
boxers, briefs	ယောက်ျားဝတ်အတွင်းခံ	jau' kja: wu' atwin: gan
panties	မိန်းကလေးဝတ်အတွင်းခံ	mein: galei: wa' atwin: gan
undershirt (A-shirt)	စွပ်ကျယ်	su' kje
socks	ခြေအိတ်များ	chei ei' mja:

nightdress	ညအိပ်ဝါဝန်ရှည်	nja a' ga wun she
bra	ဘရာစီယာ	ba ra si ja
knee highs (knee-high socks)	ခြေအိတ်ရှည်	chei ei' shi
pantyhose	အသားကပ်-ဘောင်းဘီရှည်	atha: ka' baun: bi shei
stockings (thigh highs)	စတော့ကင်	sato. kin
bathing suit	ရေကူးဝတ်စုံ	jei ku: wa' zoun

35. Headwear

hat	ဦးထုပ်	u: htou'
fedora	ဦးထုပ်ပျော့	u: htou' pjo.
baseball cap	ရှာထိုးဦးထုပ်	sha dou: u: dou'
flatcap	လှကြီးေဆာင်းဦးထုပ်ပြား	lu gji: zaun: u: dou' pja:

beret	ဘယ်ရီဦးထုပ်	be ji u: htu'
hood	အကျီတွင်ပါသော ခေါင်းစွပ်	akji. twin pa dho: gaun: zu'
panama hat	ဦးထုပ်အဝိုင်း	u: htou' awain:
knit cap (knitted hat)	သိုးမွေးခေါင်းစွပ်	thou: mwei: gaun: zu'
headscarf	ခေါင်းစည်းပုဝါ	gaun: zi: bu. wa
women's hat	အမျိုးသမီးေဆာင်း ဦးထုပ်	amjou: dhami: zaun: u: htou'

hard hat	ဦးထုပ်အမာ	u: htou' ama
garrison cap	တာပ်မတော်သုံးဦးထုပ်	ta' mado dhoun: u: dou'
helmet	အမာစားဦးထုပ်	ama za: u: htou'
derby	ဦးထုပ်လုံး	u: htou' loun:
top hat	ဦးထုပ်မြင့်	u: htou' mjin.

36. Footwear

footwear	ဖိနပ်	hpana'
shoes (men's shoes)	ရှူးဖိနပ်	shu: hpi. na'

shoes (women's shoes)	မိန်းကလေးစီးရှူးဖိနပ်	mein: galei: zi: shu: bi. na'
boots (e.g., cowboy ~)	လည်ရှည်ဖိနပ်	le she bi. na'
slippers	အိမ်တွင်းစီးကွင်းလိုးဖိနပ်	ein dwin:

tennis shoes (e.g., Nike ~)	အားကစားဖိနပ်	a: gaza: bana'
sneakers	ပတ္တူဖိနပ်	pa' tu bi. na'
(e.g., Converse ~)		
sandals	ကြိုးသိုင်းဖိနပ်	kjou: dhain: bi. na'

cobbler (shoe repairer)	ဖိနပ်ချုပ်သမား	hpana' chou' tha ma:
heel	ဒေါက်	dau'
pair (of shoes)	အစုံ	asoun.

shoestring	ဖိနပ်ကြိုး	hpana' kjou:
to lace (vt)	ဖိနပ်ကြိုးချည်သည်	hpana' kjou: gjin de
shoehorn	ဖိနပ်စီးရာသွင်းသုံး	hpana' si: ja dhwin dhoun:
	သည့် ဖိနပ်ဂေါက်	dhin. hpana' ko
shoe polish	ဖိနပ်တိုက်ဆေး	hpana' tou' hsei:

37. Personal accessories

gloves	လက်အိတ်	lei' ei'
mittens	နှစ်ကန့်လက်အိတ်	hni' kan. le' ei'
scarf (muffler)	မာဖလာ	ma ba. la

glasses (eyeglasses)	မျက်မှန်	mje' hman
frame (eyeglass ~)	မျက်မှန်ကိုင်း	mje' hman gain:
umbrella	ထီး	hti:
walking stick	တုတ်ကောက်	tou' kau'
hairbrush	ခေါင်းဘီး	gaun: bi:
fan	ပန်ကန်	pan gan

tie (necktie)	လည်စည်း	le zi:
bow tie	ဖဲပြားပုံလည်စည်း	hpe' bja: boun le zi:
suspenders	ဘောင်းဘီသိုင်းကြိုး	baun: bi dhain: gjou:
handkerchief	လက်ကိုင်ပုဝါ	le' kain bu. wa

comb	ဘီး	bi:
barrette	ဆံညှပ်	hsan hnja'

hairpin	ကလစ်	kali'
buckle	ခါးပတ်ခေါင်း	kha: ba' khaun:

belt	ခါးပတ်	kha: ba'
shoulder strap	ပုခုံးသိုင်းကြိုး	pu. goun: dhain: gjou:

bag (handbag)	လက်ကိုင်အိတ်	le' kain ei'
purse	မိန်းကလေးပုံး	mein: galei: bou goun:
	လွယ်အိတ်	lwe ei'
backpack	ကျောပိုးအိတ်	kjo: bou: ei'

38. Clothing. Miscellaneous

fashion	ဖက်ရှင်	hpe' shin
in vogue (adj)	ခေတ်မီသော	khi' mi de.
fashion designer	ဖက်ရှင်ဒီဖိုင်နာ	hpe' shin di zain na
collar	အကွီကောက်လာ	akji. ko la
pocket	အိတ်ကပ်	ei' ka'
pocket (as adj)	အိတ်ဆောင်	ei' hsaun
sleeve	အကွီလက်	akji. le'
hanging loop	အကွီချိတ်ကွင်း	akji. gjei' kwin:
fly (on trousers)	ဘောင်းဘီလျှာဆက်	baun: bi ja ze'
zipper (fastener)	ဇစ်	zi'
fastener	ချိတ်စရာ	che' zaja
button	ကြယ်သီး	kje dhi:
buttonhole	ကြယ်သီးပေါက်	kje dhi: bau'
to come off (ab. button)	ပြုတ်ထွက်သည်	pjou' htwe' te
to sew (vi, vt)	စက်ချုပ်သည်	se' khjou' te
to embroider (vi, vt)	ပန်းထိုးသည်	pan: dou: de
embroidery	ပန်းထိုးခြင်း	pan: dou: gjin:
sewing needle	အပ်	a'
thread	အပ်ချည်	a' chi
seam	ချုပ်ရိုး	chou' jou:
to get dirty (vi)	ညစ်ပေသွားသည်	nji: pei dhwa: de
stain (mark, spot)	အစွန်းအထင်း	aswan: ahtin:
to crease, crumple (vi)	တွန့်ကြေစေသည်	tun. gjei zei de
to tear, to rip (vt)	ပေါက်ပြဲသွားသည်	pau' pje: dhwa: de
clothes moth	အဝတ်ပိုးဖလံ	awu' pou: hpa. lan

39. Personal care. Cosmetics

toothpaste	သွားတိုက်ဆေး	thwa: tai' hsei:
toothbrush	သွားတိုက်တံ	thwa: tai' tan
to brush one's teeth	သွားတိုက်သည်	thwa: tai' te
razor	သင်တုန်းဓား	thin toun: da:
shaving cream	မုတ်ဆိတ်ရိတ် ဆပ်ပြာ	mou' zei' jei' hsa' pja
to shave (vi)	ရိတ်သည်	jei' te
soap	ဆပ်ပြာ	hsa' pja
shampoo	ခေါင်းလျှော်ရည်	gaun: sho je
scissors	ကတ်ကြေး	ka' kjei:
nail file	လက်သည်းတိုက်တံစင်း	le' the:
nail clippers	လက်သည်းညှပ်	le' the: hnja'
tweezers	ဇာဂနာ	za ga. na

cosmetics	အလှကုန်ပစ္စည်း	ahla. koun pji' si:
face mask	မျက်နှာပေါင်းတင်ခြင်း	mje' hna baun: din gjin:
manicure	လက်သည်းအလှပြင်ခြင်း	le' the: ahla bjin gjin
to have a manicure	လက်သည်းအလှပြင်သည်	le' the: ahla bjin de
pedicure	ခြေသည်းအလှပြင်သည်	chei dhi: ahla. pjin de
make-up bag	မိတ်ကပ်အိတ်	mi' ka' ei'
face powder	ပေါင်ဒါ	paun da
powder compact	ပေါင်ဒါဘူး	paun da bu:
blusher	ပါးနီ	pa: ni
perfume (bottled)	ရေမွှေး	jei mwei:
toilet water (lotion)	ရေမွှေး	jei mwei:
lotion	လိုးရှင်း	lou shin:
cologne	အော်ဒီကလုန်းရေမွှေး	o di ka lun: jei mwei:
eyeshadow	မျက်ခွံဆိုးဆေး	mje' khwan zou: zei:
eyeliner	အိုင်းလိုင်နာတောင့်	ain: lain: na daun.
mascara	မျက်တောင်ခြယ်ဆေး	mje' taun gje zei:
lipstick	နှုတ်ခမ်းနီ	hna' khan: ni
nail polish, enamel	လက်သည်းဆိုးဆေး	le' the: azou: zei:
hair spray	ဆံပင်သုံး စပရေး	zabin dhoun za. ba. jei:
deodorant	ချွေးနံ့ပျောက်ဆေး	chwei: nan. bjau' hsei:
cream	ခရင်မ်	khajin m
face cream	မျက်နှာခရင်မ်	mje' hna ga. jin m
hand cream	ဟန်ခရင်မ်	han kha. rin m
anti-wrinkle cream	အသားခြောက်ကာကွယ်ဆေး	atha: gjau' ka gwe zei:
day cream	နေ့လိမ်းခရင်မ်	nei. lein: ga jin'm
night cream	ညလိမ်းခရင်မ်	nja lein: khajinm
day (as adj)	နေ့လယ်ဘက်သုံးသော	nei. le be' thoun: de.
night (as adj)	ညဘက်သုံးသော	nja. be' thoun: de.
tampon	အတောင့်	ataun.
toilet paper (toilet roll)	အိမ်သာသုံးစက္ကူ	ein dha dhoun: se' ku
hair dryer	ဆံပင်အခြောက်ခံစက်	zabin achou' hsan za'

40. Watches. Clocks

watch (wristwatch)	နာရီ	na ji
dial	နာရီဒိုက်ရွက်	na ji dai' hpwe'
hand (of clock, watch)	နာရီလက်တံ	na ji le' tan
metal watch band	နာရီကြိုး	na ji gjou:
watch strap	နာရီကြိုး	na ji gjou:
battery	ဘတ်ခဲ	da' khe:
to be dead (battery)	အားကုန်သည်	a: kun de
to change a battery	ဘတ်ထရီလဲသည်	ba' hta ji le: de
to run fast	မြန်သည်	mjan de

to run slow	နောက်ကျသည်	nau' kja. de
wall clock	တိုင်ကပ်နာရီ	tain ka' na ji
hourglass	သဲနာရီ	the: naji
sundial	နေနာရီ	nei na ji
alarm clock	နှိုးစက်	hnou: ze'
watchmaker	နာရီပြင်ဆဝရာ	ma ji bjin zaja
to repair (vt)	ပြင်သည်	pjin de

EVERYDAY EXPERIENCE

41. Money

money	ပိုက်ဆံ	pai' hsan
currency exchange	လဲလှယ်ခြင်း	le: hle gjin:
exchange rate	ငွေလဲနန်း	ngwei le: hnan:
ATM	အလိုအလျောက်ငွေထုတ်စက်	alou aljau' ngwei htou' se'
coin	အကြွေစေ့	akjwei zei.

| dollar | ဒေါ်လာ | do la |
| euro | ယူရို | ju rou |

lira	အီတလီ လိုင်ရာငွေ	ita. li lain ja ngwei
Deutschmark	ဂျာမန်မတ်ငွေ	gja man ma' ngwei
franc	ဖရန့်	hpa. jan.
pound sterling	စတာလင်ပေါင်	sata lin baun
yen	ယန်း	jan:

debt	အကြွေး	akjwei:
debtor	မြီစား	mji za:
to lend (money)	ရေးသည်	chei: de
to borrow (vi, vt)	အကြွေးယူသည်	akjwei: ju de

bank	ဘက်	ban
account	ငွေစာရင်း	ngwei za jin:
to deposit (vt)	ထည့်သည်	hte de.
to deposit into the account	ငွေသွင်းသည်	ngwei dhwin: de
to withdraw (vt)	ငွေထုတ်သည်	ngwei dou' te

credit card	အကြွေးဝယ်ကဒ်ပြား	akjwei: we ka' pja
cash	လက်ငင်း	le' ngin:
check	ချက်	che'
to write a check	ချက်ရေးသည်	che' jei: de
checkbook	ချက်စာအုပ်	che' sa ou'

wallet	ပိုက်ဆံအိတ်	pai' hsan ei'
change purse	ပိုက်ဆံအိတ်	pai' hsan ei'
safe	မီးခံသေတ္တာ	mi: gan dhi' ta

heir	အမွေစားအမွေခံ	amwei za: amwei gan
inheritance	အမွေဆက်ခံခြင်း	amwei ze' khan gjin:
fortune (wealth)	အခွင့်အလမ်း	akhwin. alan:

| lease | အိမ်ငှား | ein hnga: |
| rent (money) | အခန်းငှားခ | akhan: hnga: ga |

to rent (sth from sb)	ငှားသည်	hnga: de
price	ဈေးနှုန်း	zei: hnan:
cost	ကုန်ကျစရိတ်	koun gja. za. ji'
sum	ပေါင်းလဒ်	paun: la'

to spend (vt)	သုံးစွဲသည်	thoun: zwe: de
expenses	စရိတ်စက	zaei' zaga.
to economize (vi, vt)	ချွေတာသည်	chwei da de
economical	တွက်ခြေကိုက်သော	twe' chei kai' te.

to pay (vi, vt)	ပေးချေသည်	pei: gjei de
payment	ပေးချေသည့်ငွေ	pei: gjei de. ngwei
change (give the ~)	ပြန်အမ်းငွေ	pjan an: ngwe

tax	အခွန်	akhun
fine	ဒဏ်ငွေ	dan ngwei
to fine (vt)	ဒဏ်ရိုက်သည်	dan jai' de

42. Post. Postal service

post office	စာတိုက်	sa dai'
mail (letters, etc.)	မေးလ်	mei: l
mailman	စာပို့သမား	sa bou. dhama:
opening hours	ဖွင့်ချိန်	hpwin. gjin

letter	စာ	sa
registered letter	မှတ်ပုံတင်ပြီးသောစာ	hma' poun din bji: dho: za:
postcard	ပို့စ်ကတ်	pou. sa. ka'
telegram	ကြေးနန်း	kjei: nan:
package (parcel)	ပါဆယ်	pa ze
money transfer	ငွေလွှဲခြင်း	ngwei hlwe: gjin:

to receive (vt)	လက်ခံရရှိသည်	le' khan ja. shi. de
to send (vt)	ပို့သည်	pou. de
sending	ပို့ခြင်း	pou. gjin:

address	လိပ်စာ	lei' sa
ZIP code	စာပို့သင်္ကေတ	sa bou dhin kei ta.
sender	ပို့သူ	pou. dhu
receiver	လက်ခံသူ	le' khan dhu

name (first name)	အမည်	amji
surname (last name)	မိသားစု မျိုး ရိုးနာမည်	mi. dha: zu. mjou: jou: na mji

postage rate	စာပို့ခ နှုန်းထား	sa bou. kha. hnan: da:
standard (adj)	စံနှုန်းသတ်မှတ် ထား:သော	san hnoun: dha' hma' hta: de.
economical (adj)	ကုန်ကျငွေသက် သာ:သော	koun gja ngwe dhe' dha de.

weight	အလေးချိန်	alei: gjein
to weigh (~ letters)	ချိန်သည်	chein de
envelope	စာအိတ်	sa ei'
postage stamp	တံဆိပ်ခေါင်း	da zei' khaun:
to stamp an envelope	တံဆိပ်ခေါင်းကပ်သည်	da zei' khaun: ka' te

43. Banking

bank	ဘဏ်	ban
branch (of bank, etc.)	ဘဏ်ခွဲ	ban gwe:
bank clerk, consultant	အတိုင်ပင်ခံပုဂ္ဂိုလ်	atain bin gan bou' gou
manager (director)	မန်နေဂျာ	man nei gji
bank account	ဘဏ်ငွေစာရင်း	ban ngwei za jin
account number	ဘဏ်စာရင်းနံပါတ်	ban zajin: nan. ba'
checking account	ဘဏ်စာရင်းရှင်	ban zajin: shin
savings account	ဘဏ်ငွေစုစာရင်း	ban ngwei zu. za jin
to open an account	ဘဏ်စာရင်းဖွင့်သည်	ban zajin: hpwin. de
to close the account	ဘဏ်စာရင်းပိတ်သည်	ban zajin: bi' te
to deposit into the account	ငွေသွင်းသည်	ngwei dhwin: de
to withdraw (vt)	ငွေထုတ်သည်	ngwei dou' te
deposit	အပ်ငွေ	a' ngwei
to make a deposit	ငွေအပ်သည်	ngwei a' te
wire transfer	ကြေးနန်းဖြင့်ငွေလွှဲခြင်း	kjei: nan: bjin. ngwe hlwe: gjin
to wire, to transfer	ကြေးနန်းဖြင့် ငွေလွှဲသည်	kjei: nan: bjin. ngwe hlwe: de
sum	ပေါင်းလဒ်	paun: la'
How much?	ဘယ်လောက်လဲ	be lau' le:
signature	လက်မှတ်	le' hma'
to sign (vt)	လက်မှတ်ထိုးသည်	le' hma' htou: de
credit card	အကြွေးဝယ်ကဒ်- ရက္ခဒစ်ကဒ်	achwei: we ka' - ka' je' da' ka'
code (PIN code)	ကုဒ်နံပါတ်	kou' nan ba'
credit card number	ရက္ခဒစ်ကဒ်နံပါတ်	kha. je' di' ka' nan ba'
ATM	အလိုအလျောက်ငွေထုတ်စက်	alou aljau' ngwei htou' se'
check	ချက်လက်မှတ်	che' le' hma'
to write a check	ချက်ရေးသည်	che' jei: de
checkbook	ချက်စာအုပ်	che' sa ou'
loan (bank ~)	ချေးငွေ	chei: ngwei
to apply for a loan	ချေးငွေလျှောက် လွှာတင်သည်	chei: ngwei shau' hlwa din de

to get a loan	ချေးငွေရယူသည်	chei: ngwei ja. ju de
to give a loan	ချေးငွေထုတ်ပေးသည်	chei: ngwei htou' pei: de
guarantee	အာမခံပစ္စည်း	a ma. gan bji' si:

44. Telephone. Phone conversation

telephone	တယ်လီဖုန်း	te li hpoun:
cell phone	မိုဘိုင်းဖုန်း	mou bain: hpoun:
answering machine	ဖုန်းထူးစက်	hpoun: du: ze'
to call (by phone)	ဖုန်းဆက်သည်	hpoun: ze' te
phone call	အဝင်ဖုန်း	awin hpun:
to dial a number	နံပါတ် နှိပ်သည်	nan ba' hnei' te
Hello!	ဟာလို	ha. lou
to ask (vt)	မေးသည်	mei: de
to answer (vi, vt)	ဖြေသည်	hpjei de
to hear (vt)	ကြားသည်	ka: de
well (adv)	ကောင်းကောင်း	kaun: gaun:
not well (adv)	အရမ်းမကောင်း	ajan: ma. gaun:
noises (interference)	ဖြတ်ဝင်သည့်ဆူညံသံ	hpja' win dhi. zu njan dhan
receiver	တယ်လီဖုန်းနားကြပ်ပိုင်း	te li hpoun: na: gja' pain:
to pick up (~ the phone)	ဖုန်းကောက်ကိုင်သည်	hpoun: gau' gain de
to hang up (~ the phone)	ဖုန်းချသည်	hpoun: gja de
busy (engaged)	လိုင်းမအားသော	lain: ma. a: de.
to ring (ab. phone)	မြည်သည်	mji de
telephone book	တယ်လီဖုန်းလမ်း	te li hpoun: lan:
	ညွှန်စာအုပ်	hnjun za ou'
local (adj)	ပြည်တွင်းဒေသ	pji dwin: dei. dha
	တွင်းဖြစ်သော	dwin: bji' te.
local call	ပြည်တွင်းခေါ်ဆိုမှု	pji dwin: go zou hmu.
long distance (~ call)	အဝေးခေါ်ဆိုနိုင်သော	awei: go zou nain de.
long-distance call	အဝေးခေါ်ဆိုမှု	awei: go zou hmu.
international (adj)	အပြည်ပြည်ဆိုင်ရာဖြစ်သော	apji pji zain ja bja' de.
international call	အပြည်ပြည်ဆိုင်ရာခေါ်ဆိုမှု	apji pji zain ja go: zou hmu

45. Cell phone

cell phone	မိုဘိုင်းဖုန်း	mou bain: hpoun:
display	ပြသခြင်း	pja. dha. gjin:
button	လေ့လုတ်	khalou'
SIM card	ဆင်းကဒ်	hsin: ka'
battery	ဘတ်ထရီ	ba' hta ji
to be dead (battery)	ဖုန်းအားကုန်သည်	hpoun: a: goun: de

charger	အားသွင်းကြိုး	a: dhwin: gjou:
menu	အစားအသောက်စာရင်း	asa: athau' sa jin:
settings	ချိန်ညှိခြင်း	chein hnji. chin:
tune (melody)	တီးလုံး	ti: loun:
to select (vt)	ရွေးချယ်သည်	jwei: che de

calculator	ဂဏန်းပေါင်းစက်	ganan: baun: za'
voice mail	အသံမေးလ်	athan mei:l
alarm clock	နှိုးစက်	hnou: ze'
contacts	ဖုန်းအဆက်အသွယ်များ	hpoun: ase' athwe mja:

| SMS (text message) | မက်ဆေ့ဂျ် | me' zei. gja |
| subscriber | အသုံးပြုသူ | athoun: bju. dhu |

46. Stationery

| ballpoint pen | ဘောပင် | bo pin |
| fountain pen | ဖောင်တိန် | hpaun din |

pencil	ခဲတံ	khe: dan
highlighter	အရောင်တောက်မင်တံ	ajaun dau' min dan
felt-tip pen	ရေဆေးစုတ်တံ	jei zei: zou' tan

| notepad | မှတ်စုစာအုပ် | hma' su. za ou' |
| agenda (diary) | နေ့စဉ်မှတ်တမ်းစာအုပ် | nei. zin hma' tan: za ou' |

ruler	ပေတံ	pei dan
calculator	ဂဏန်းပေါင်းစက်	ganan: baun: za'
eraser	ခဲဖျက်	khe: bje'
thumbtack	ထိပ်ပြားကြီးသံမှို	htei' pja: gji: dhan hmou
paper clip	တွယ်ချိတ်	twe gjei'

glue	ကော်	ko
stapler	စတက်ပလာ	sate' pa. la
hole punch	အပေါက်ဖောက်စက်	apau' hpau' se'
pencil sharpener	ခဲချွန်စက်	khe: chun ze'

47. Foreign languages

language	ဘာသာစကား	ba dha zaga:
foreign (adj)	နိုင်ငံခြားနှင့် သိုင်သော	nain ngan gja: hnin. zain de.
foreign language	နိုင်ငံခြားဘာ သာစကား	nain ngan gja: ba dha za ga:
to study (vt)	သင်ယူလေ့လာသည်	thin ju lei. la de
to learn (language, etc.)	သင်ယူသည်	thin ju de
to read (vi, vt)	ဖတ်သည်	hpa' te
to speak (vi, vt)	ပြောသည်	pjo: de

to understand (vt)	နားလည်သည်	na: le de
to write (vt)	ရေးသည်	jei' de
fast (adv)	မြန်မြန်	mjan mjan
slowly (adv)	ဖြည်းဖြည်း	hpjei: bjei:
fluently (adv)	ကျွမ်းကျွမ်းကျင်ကျင်	kjwan: gjwan: gjin gjin
rules	စည်းမျဉ်းစည်းကမ်း	si: mjin: si: kan:
grammar	သဒ္ဒါ	dhada
vocabulary	ဝေါဟာရ	wo: ha ra.
phonetics	သဒ္ဒဗေဒ	dhada. bei da.
textbook	ဖတ်စာအုပ်	hpa' sa au'
dictionary	အဘိဓာန်	abi. dan
teach-yourself book	မိမိဘာသာလေ့ လာနိုင်သောစာအုပ်	mi. mi. ba dha lei. la nain dho: za ou'
phrasebook	နှစ်ဘာသာစွဲစကား မြောစာအုပ်	hni' ba dha zaga: bjo: za ou'
cassette, tape	တိပ်ခွေ	tei' khwei
videotape	ရုပ်ရှင်တိပ်ခွေ	jou' shin dei' hpwei
CD, compact disc	စီဒီခွေ	si di gwei
DVD	ဒီဗီဒီခွေ	di bi di gwei
alphabet	အက္ခရာ	e' kha ja
to spell (vt)	စာလုံးပေါင်းသည်	sa loun: baun: de
pronunciation	အသံထွက်	athan dwe'
accent	ဝဲသံ	we: dhan
with an accent	ဝဲသံနှင့်	we: dhan hnin.
without an accent	ဝဲသံမပါဘဲ	we: dhan ma. ba be:
word	စကားလုံး	zaga: loun:
meaning	အဓိပ္ပါယ်	adei' be
course (e.g., a French ~)	သင်တန်း	thin dan:
to sign up	စာရင်းသွင်းသည်	sajin: dhwin: de
teacher	ဆရာ	hsa ja
translation (process)	ဘာသာပြန်ခြင်း	ba dha bjan gjin:
translation (text, etc.)	ဘာသာပြန်ထားချက်	ba dha bjan da: gje'
translator	ဘာသာပြန်	ba dha bjan
interpreter	စကားပြန်	zaga: bjan
polyglot	ဘာသာစကားအများ ပြောနိုင်သူ	ba dha zaga: amja: bjo: nain dhu
memory	မှတ်ညဏ်	hma' njan

MEALS. RESTAURANT

48. Table setting

spoon	ဇွန်း	zun:
knife	ဓား	da:
fork	ခက်ရင်း	khajin:
cup (e.g., coffee ~)	ခွက်	khwe'
plate (dinner ~)	ပန်းကန်ပြား	bagan: bja:
saucer	အောက်ခံပန်းကန်ပြား	au' khan ban: kan pja:
napkin (on table)	လက်သုတ်ပုဝါ	le' thou' pu. wa
toothpick	သွားကြားထိုးတံ	thwa: kja: dou: dan

49. Restaurant

restaurant	စားသောက်ဆိုင်	sa: thau' hsain
coffee house	ကော်ဖီဆိုင်	ko hpi zain
pub, bar	ဘား	ba:
tearoom	လက်ဖက်ရည်ဆိုင်	le' hpe' ji zain
waiter	စားပွဲထိုး	sa: bwe: dou:
waitress	စားပွဲထိုးမိန်းကလေး	sa: bwe: dou: mein: ga. lei:
bartender	အရက်ဘားဝန်ထမ်း	aje' ba: wun dan:
menu	စားသောက်ဖွယ်စာရင်း	sa: thau' hpwe za jin:
wine list	ဝိုင်စာရင်း	wain za jin:
to book a table	စားပွဲကြိုတင် မှာယူသည်	sa: bwe: gjou din hma ju de
course, dish	ဟင်းပွဲ	hin: bwe:
to order (meal)	မှာသည်	hma de
to make an order	မှာသည်	hma de
aperitif	နှုတ်မြိန်ဆေး	hna' mjein zei:
appetizer	နှုတ်မြိန်စာ	hna' mjein za
dessert	အချိုပွဲ	achou bwe:
check	ကျသင့်ငွေ	kja. thin. ngwei
to pay the check	ကုန်ကျငွေရှင်းသည်	koun gja ngwei shin: de
to give change	ပြန်အမ်းသည်	pjan an: de
tip	မုန့်ဖိုး	moun. bou:

50. Meals

food	အစားအစာ	asa: asa
to eat (vi, vt)	စားသည်	sa: de
breakfast	နံနက်စာ	nan ne' za
to have breakfast	နံနက်စာစားသည်	nan ne' za za: de
lunch	နေ့လယ်စာ	nei. le za
to have lunch	နေ့လယ်စာစားသည်	nei. le za za de
dinner	ညစာ	nja. za
to have dinner	ညစာစားသည်	nja. za za: de
appetite	စားချင်စိတ်	sa: gjin zei'
Enjoy your meal!	စားကောင်းပါစေ	sa: gaun: ba zei
to open (~ a bottle)	ဖွင့်သည်	hpwin. de
to spill (liquid)	ဖိတ်ကျသည်	hpi' kja de
to spill out (vi)	မှောက်သည်	hmau' de
to boil (vi)	ဆူပွက်သည်	hsu. bwe' te
to boil (vt)	ဆူပွက်သည်	hsu. bwe' te
boiled (~ water)	ဆူပွက်ထားသော	hsu. bwe' hta: de.
to chill, cool down (vt)	အအေးခံသည်	aei: gan de
to chill (vi)	အေးသွားသည်	ei: dhwa: de
taste, flavor	အရသာ	aja. dha
aftertaste	ပအာခြင်း	pa. achin:
to slim down (lose weight)	ဖိတ်ချသည်	wei' cha. de
diet	ဓာတ်စာ	da' sa
vitamin	ဗီတာမင်	bi ta min
calorie	ကယ်လိုရီ	ke lou ji
vegetarian (n)	သက်သက်လွတ်စားသူ	the' the' lu' za: dhu
vegetarian (adj)	သက်သက်လွတ်စားသော	the' the' lu' za: de.
fats (nutrient)	အဆီ	ahsi
proteins	အသားဓာတ်	atha: da'
carbohydrates	ကစီဓာတ်	ka. zi da'
slice (of lemon, ham)	အရပ်	acha'
piece (of cake, pie)	အတုံး	atoun:
crumb	အစအန	asa an
(of bread, cake, etc.)		

51. Cooked dishes

course, dish	ဟင်းပွဲ	hin: bwe:
cuisine	အစားအသောက်	asa: athau'
recipe	ဟင်းချက်နည်း	hin: gji' ne:

portion	တစ်ယောက်စာဟင်းပွဲ	ti' jau' sa hin: bwe:
salad	အသုပ်	athou'
soup	စွပ်ပြုတ်	su' pjou'
clear soup (broth)	ဟင်းရည်	hin: ji
sandwich (bread)	အသားညှပ်ပေါင်မုန့်	atha: hnja' paun moun.
fried eggs	ကြက်ဥကြော်	kje' u. kjo
hamburger (beefburger)	ဟန်ဘာဂါ	han ba ga
beefsteak	အမဲသားတုံး	ame: dha: doun:
side dish	အရံဟင်း	ajan hin:
spaghetti	အီတာလီခေါက်ဆွဲ	ita. li khau' hswe:
mashed potatoes	အာလူးနွားနို့ဖျော်	a luu: nwa: nou. bjo
pizza	ပီဇာ	pi za
porridge (oatmeal, etc.)	အုတ်ဂျူးယာဂု	ou' gjoun ja gu.
omelet	ကြက်ဥခေါက်ကြော်	kje' u. khau' kjo
boiled (e.g., ~ beef)	ပြုတ်ထားသော	pjou' hta: de.
smoked (adj)	ကင်တင်ထားသော	kja' tin da: de.
fried (adj)	ကြော်ထားသော	kjo da de.
dried (adj)	ခြောက်နေသော	chau' nei de.
frozen (adj)	အေးခဲနေသော	ei: khe: nei de.
pickled (adj)	သားရည်စိမ်ထားသော	hsa:
sweet (sugary)	ချိုသော	chou de.
salty (adj)	ငန်သော	ngan de.
cold (adj)	အေးသော	ei: de.
hot (adj)	ပူသော	pu dho:
bitter (adj)	ခါးသော	kha: de.
tasty (adj)	အရသာရှိသော	aja. dha shi. de.
to cook in boiling water	ပြုတ်သည်	pjou' te
to cook (dinner)	ချက်သည်	che' de
to fry (vt)	ကြော်သည်	kjo de
to heat up (food)	အပူပေးသည်	apu bei: de
to salt (vt)	သားထည့်သည်	hsa: hte. de
to pepper (vt)	အစပ်ထည့်သည်	asin hte. dhe
to grate (vt)	ခြစ်သည်	chi' te
peel (n)	အခွံ	akhun
to peel (vt)	အခွံနွာသည်	akhun hnwa de

52. Food

meat	အသား	atha:
chicken	ကြက်သား	kje' tha:
Rock Cornish hen (poussin)	ကြက်ကလေး	kje' ka. lei:
duck	ဘဲသား	be: dha:

goose	ဘဲငန်းသား	be: ngan: dha:
game	တောကောင်သား	to: gaun dha:
turkey	ကြက်ဆင်သား	kje' hsin dha:
pork	ဝက်သား	we' tha:
veal	နွားကလေးသား	nwa: ga. lei: dha:
lamb	သိုးသား	thou: tha:
beef	အမဲသား	ame: dha:
rabbit	ယုန်သား	joun dha:
sausage (bologna, etc.)	ဝက်အူချောင်း	we' u gjaun:
vienna sausage (frankfurter)	အသားချောင်း	atha: gjaun:
bacon	ဝက်ဆားနယ်ခြောက်	we' has: ne gjau'
ham	ဝက်ပေါင်ခြောက်	we' paun gjau'
gammon	ဝက်ပေါင်ကြက်တိုက်	we' paun gje' tai'
pâté	အနှစ်အခဲပျော့	ahni' akhe pjo.
liver	အသည်း	athe:
hamburger (ground beef)	ကြိတ်သား	kjei' tha:
tongue	လျှာ	sha
egg	ဥ	u.
eggs	ဥများ	u. mja:
egg white	အကာ	aka
egg yolk	အနှစ်	ahni'
fish	ငါး	nga:
seafood	ပင်လယ်အစားအစာ	pin le asa: asa
crustaceans	အခွံမာရေနေ သတ္တဝါ	akhun ma jei nei dha' ta. wa
caviar	ငါးဥ	nga: u.
crab	ကဏန်း	kanan:
shrimp	ပုစွန်	bazun
oyster	ကမာကောင်	kama kaun
spiny lobster	ကျောက်ပုစွန်	kjau' pu. zun
octopus	ရေဘဝဲသား	jei ba. we: dha:
squid	ပြည်ကြီးငါး	pjei gji: nga:
sturgeon	စတာဂျင်ငါး	sata gjin nga:
salmon	ဆော်လမွန်ငါး	hso: la. mun nga:
halibut	ပင်လယ်ငါးကြီးသား	pin le nga: gji: dha:
cod	ငါးကြီးဆီထုတ်သောငါး	nga: gji: zi dou' de. nga:
mackerel	မက်ကရယ်ငါး	me' ka. je nga:
tuna	တူနာငါး	tu na nga:
eel	ငါးရှဉ့်	nga: shin.
trout	ထရောက်ငါး	hta. jau' nga:
sardine	ငါးသေတ္တာငါး	nga: dhei ta' nga:
pike	ပိုက်ငါး	pai' nga

herring	ငါးသလောက်	nga: dha. lau'
bread	ပေါင်မုန့်	paun moun.
cheese	ဒိန်ခဲ	dain ge:
sugar	သကြား	dhagja:
salt	ဆား	hsa:

rice	ဆန်စပါး	hsan zaba
pasta (macaroni)	အီတာလီခေါက်ဆွဲ	ita. li khau' hswe:
noodles	ခေါက်ဆွဲ	gau' hswe:

butter	ထောပတ်	hto: ba'
vegetable oil	ဆီ	hsi
sunflower oil	နေကြာပန်းဆီ	nei gja ban: zi
margarine	ဟင်းရွက်အဆီခဲ	hin: jwe' ahsi khe:

| olives | သံလွင်သီး | than lun dhi: |
| olive oil | သံလွင်ဆီ | than lun zi |

milk	နွားနို့	nwa: nou.
condensed milk	နို့ဆီ	ni. zi
yogurt	ဒိန်ချဉ်	dain gjin
sour cream	နို့ချဉ်	nou. gjin
cream (of milk)	မလိုင်	ma. lain

| mayonnaise | ဝပ်ပျစ်ပျစ်စားမြိန်ရည် | kha' pji' pji' sa: mjein jei |
| buttercream | ထောပတ်မလိုင် | hto: ba' ma. lein |

groats (barley ~, etc.)	နံစားဇေ၀	nhnan za: zei.
flour	ဂျုံမုန့်	gjoun hmoun.
canned food	စည်သွပ်ပုံးများ	si dhwa' bu: mja:

cornflakes	ပြောင်းဖူးမုန့်ဆန်း	pjaun: bu: moun. zan:
honey	ပျားရည်	pja: je
jam	ယို	jou
chewing gum	ပီကေ	pi gei

53. Drinks

water	ရေ	jei
drinking water	သောက်ရေ	thau' jei
mineral water	ဓာတ်ဆားရည်	da' hsa: ji

still (adj)	ဂတ်စ်မပါသော	ga' s ma. ba de.
carbonated (adj)	ဂတ်စ်ပါသော	ga' s ba de.
sparkling (adj)	စပါကလင်	saba ga. lin
ice	ရေခဲ	jei ge:
with ice	ရေခဲနှင့်	jei ge: hnin.
non-alcoholic (adj)	အယ်ကိုဟောမပါသော	e kou ho: ma. ba de.
soft drink	အယ်ကိုဟောမှဟုတ်သော သောက်စရာ	e kou ho: ma. hou' te. dhau' sa. ja

refreshing drink	အအေး	aei:
lemonade	လီမွန်ဖျော်ရည်	li mun hpjo ji
liquors	အယ်ကိုဟောႏပါဝင်သော သောက်စရာ	e kou ho: ba win de. dhau' sa. ja
wine	ဝိုင်	wain
white wine	ဝိုင်ဖြူ	wain gju
red wine	ဝိုင်နီ	wain ni
liqueur	အရက်ချိုပြင်း	aje' gjou pjin
champagne	ရှန်ပိန်	shan pein
vermouth	ရန့်သင်းဒွှော ဇေးစိမ်ဝိုင်	jan dhin: dho: zei: zein wain
whiskey	ဝီစကီ	wi sa. gi
vodka	ဗော့ကာ	bo ga
gin	ဂျင်	gjin
cognac	ကော့ညက်	ko. nja'
rum	ရမ်	ran
coffee	ကော်ဖီ	ko hpi
black coffee	ဘလက်ကော်ဖီ	ba. le' ko: phi
coffee with milk	ကော်ဖီနို့ရော	ko hpi ni. jo:
cappuccino	ကပူရှီနို	ka. pu chi ni.
instant coffee	ကော်ဖီမစ်	ko hpi mi'
milk	နွားနို့	nwa: nou.
cocktail	ကော့တေး	ko. dei:
milkshake	မစ်ရှိက်	mi' shei'
juice	အချိုရည်	achou ji
tomato juice	ခရမ်းချဉ်သီးအချိုရည်	khajan: chan dhi: achou jei
orange juice	လိမ္မော်ရည်	limmo ji
freshly squeezed juice	အသီးဖျော်ရည်	athi: hpjo je
beer	ဘီယာ	bi ja
light beer	အရောင်ဖျော့သောဘီယာ	ajaun bjau. de. bi ja
dark beer	အရောင်ရင့်သောဘီယာ	ajaun jin. de. bi ja
tea	လက်ဖက်ရည်	le' hpe' ji
black tea	လက်ဖက်နက်	le' hpe' ne'
green tea	လက်ဖက်စိမ်း	le' hpe' sein:

54. Vegetables

vegetables	ဟင်းသီးဟင်းရွက်	hin: dhi: hin: jwe'
greens	ဟင်းခတ်အမွှေးရွက်	hin: ga' ahmwei: jwe'
tomato	ခရမ်းချဉ်သီး	khajan: chan dhi:
cucumber	သခွားသီး	thakhwa: dhi:

carrot	မုန်လာဥနီ	moun la u. ni
potato	အာလူး	a lu:
onion	ကြက်သွန်နီ	kje' thwan ni
garlic	ကြက်သွန်ဖြူ	kje' thwan bju

cabbage	ဂေါ်ဖီ	go bi
cauliflower	ပန်းဂေါ်ဖီ	pan: gozi
Brussels sprouts	ဂေါ်ဖီထုပ်အသေးစား	go bi dou' athei: za:
broccoli	ပန်းဂေါ်ဖီအစိမ်း	pan: gozi asein:

beet	မုန်လာဥနီလုံး	moun la u. ni loun:
eggplant	ခရမ်းသီး	khajan: dhi:
zucchini	ဘူးသီး	bu: dhi:
pumpkin	ဖရုံသီး	hpa joun dhi:
turnip	တရုတ်မုန်လာဥ	tajou' moun la u.

parsley	တရုတ်နံနံပင်	tajou' nan nan bin
dill	စမြိတ်ပင်	samjei' pin
lettuce	ဆလတ်ရွက်	hsa. la' jwe'
celery	တရုတ်နံနံကြီး	tajou' nan nan gji:
asparagus	ကညွတ်မာပင်	ka. nju' ma bin
spinach	ဒေါက်ခွ	dau' khwa.

pea	ပဲစေ့	pe: zei.
beans	ပဲအမျိုးမျိုး	pe: amjou: mjou:
corn (maize)	ပြောင်းဖူး	pjaun: bu:
kidney bean	ပဲလေးစားပဲ	bou za: be:

bell pepper	ငရုတ်သီး	nga jou' thi:
radish	မုန်လာဥသေး	moun la u. dhei:
artichoke	အာတီချော့	a ti cho.

55. Fruits. Nuts

fruit	အသီး	athi:
apple	ပန်းသီး	pan: dhi:
pear	သစ်တော်သီး	thi' to dhi:
lemon	သံပုရိုသီး	than bu. jou dhi:
orange	လိမ္မော်သီး	limmo dhi:
strawberry (garden ~)	စတော်ဘယ်ရီသီး	sato be ri dhi:

mandarin	ပျားလိမ္မော်သီး	pja: lein mo dhi:
plum	ဆီးသီး	hsi: dhi:
peach	မက်မွန်သီး	me' mwan dhi:
apricot	တရုတ်ဆီးသီး	jau' hsi: dhi:
raspberry	ရက်စဘာယ်ရီ	re' sa be ji
pineapple	နာနတ်သီး	na na' dhi:

banana	ငှက်ပျောသီး	hnge' pjo: dhi:
watermelon	ဖရဲသီး	hpa. je: dhi:

grape	စပျစ်သီး	zabji' thi:
cherry	ချယ်ရီသီး	che ji dhi:
sour cherry	ချယ်ရီချဉ်သီး	che ji gjin dhi:
sweet cherry	ချယ်ရီချိုသီး	che ji gjou dhi:
melon	သခွားမွှေးသီး	thakhwa: hmwei: dhi:

grapefruit	ဂရိတ်ဖရူသီး	ga. ri' hpa. ju dhi:
avocado	ထောပတ်သီး	hto: ba' thi:
papaya	သင်္ဘောသီး	thin: bo: dhi:
mango	သရက်သီး	thaje' thi:
pomegranate	တလည်းသီး	tale: dhi:

redcurrant	အနီရောင်ဘယ်ရီသီး	ani jaun be ji dhi:
blackcurrant	ဘလက်ကားရန့်	ba. le' ka: jan.
gooseberry	ကလားဆီးဖြူ	ka. la: his: hpju
bilberry	ဘီဘယ်ရီအသီး	bi: be ji athi:
blackberry	ရှမ်းဆီးသီး	shan: zi: di:

raisin	စပျစ်သီးခြောက်	zabji' thi: gjau'
fig	သဖန်းသီး	thahpjan: dhi:
date	စွန်ပလွံသီး	sun palun dhi:

peanut	မြေပဲ	mjei be:
almond	ဗာဒံသီး	ba dan di:
walnut	သစ်ကြားသီး	thi' kja: dhi:
hazelnut	ဟောဇယ်သီး	ho: ze dhi:
coconut	အုန်းသီး	aun: dhi:
pistachios	ခွမာသီး	khwan ma dhi:

56. Bread. Candy

bakers' confectionery (pastry)	မုန့်ရှို	moun. gjou
bread	ပေါင်မုန့်	paun moun.
cookies	ဘီစကစ်	bi za. ki'

chocolate (n)	ချောကလက်	cho: ka. le'
chocolate (as adj)	ချောကလက်အရ သာရှိသော	cho: ka. le' aja. dha shi. de.
candy (wrapped)	သကြားလုံး	dhagja: loun:
cake (e.g., cupcake)	ကိတ်	kei'
cake (e.g., birthday ~)	ကိတ်မုန့်	kei' moun.
pie (e.g., apple ~)	ပိုင်မုန့်	pain hmoun.
filling (for cake, pie)	သွပ်ထားသောအစာ	thu' hta: dho: asa

jam (whole fruit jam)	ယို	jou
marmalade	အထူးပြုလုပ်ထားသော ယို	a htu: bju. lou' hta: de. jou
wafers	ဝေဖာ	wei hpa
ice-cream	ရေခဲမုန့်	jei ge: moun.
pudding	ပူတင်း	pu tin:

57. Spices

salt	ဆား	hsa:
salty (adj)	ငန်သော	ngan de.
to salt (vt)	ဆားထည့်သည်	hsa: hte. de
black pepper	ငရုတ်ကောင်း	nga jou' kaun:
red pepper (milled ~)	ငရုတ်သီး	nga jou' thi:
mustard	မုန်ညင်း	moun njin:
horseradish	သင်္ဘောဒန့်သလွန်	thin: bo: dan. dha lun
condiment	ဟင်းခတ်အမှုန့် အမျိုးမျိုး	hin: ga' ahnun. amjou: mjou:
spice	ဟင်းခတ်အမွှေးအကြိုင်	hin: ga' ahmwei: akjain
sauce	ဆော့	hso.
vinegar	ရှာလကာရည်	sha la. ga je
anise	စမုန်စပါးပင်	samoun zaba: bin
basil	ပင်စိမ်း	pin zein:
cloves	လေးညှင်း	lei: hnjin:
ginger	ဂျင်း	gjin:
coriander	နံနံပင်	nan nan bin
cinnamon	သစ်ကြံပိုးခေါက်	thi' kjan bou: gau'
sesame	နှမ်း	hnan:
bay leaf	ကရဝေးရွက်	ka ja wei: jwe'
paprika	ပန်းငရုတ်မှုန့်	pan: nga. jou' hnoun.
caraway	ကရဝေး	ka. ja. wei:
saffron	ကုံကုမံ	koun kou man

PERSONAL INFORMATION. FAMILY

58. Personal information. Forms

name (first name)	အမည်	amji
surname (last name)	မိသားစုအမည်	mi. dha: zu. amji
date of birth	မွေးနေ့	mwei: nei.
place of birth	မွေးရပ်	mwer: ja'
nationality	လူမျိုး	lu mjou:
place of residence	နေရပ်ဒေသ	nei ja' da. dha.
country	နိုင်ငံ	nain ngan
profession (occupation)	အလုပ်အကိုင်	alou' akain
gender, sex	လိင်	lin
height	အရပ်	aja'
weight	ကိုယ်အလေးချိန်	kou alei: chain

59. Family members. Relatives

mother	အမေ	amei
father	အဖေ	ahpei
son	သား	tha:
daughter	သမီး	thami:
younger daughter	သမီးအငယ်	thami: ange
younger son	သားအငယ်	tha: ange
eldest daughter	သမီးအကြီး	thami: akji:
eldest son	သားအကြီး	tha: akji:
brother	ညီအစ်ကို	nji a' kou
elder brother	အစ်ကို	akou
younger brother	ညီ	nji
sister	ညီအစ်မ	nji a' ma
elder sister	အစ်မ	ama.
younger sister	ညီမ	nji ma.
cousin (masc.)	ဝမ်းကွဲအစ်ကို	wan: kwe: i' kou
cousin (fem.)	ဝမ်းကွဲညီမ	wan: kwe: nji ma.
mom, mommy	မေမေ	mei mei
dad, daddy	ဖေဖေ	hpei hpei
parents	မိဘတွေ	mi. ba. dwei
child	ကလေး	kalei:

children	ကလေးများ	kalei: mja:
grandmother	အဘွား	ahpwa
grandfather	အဘိုး	ahpou:
grandson	မြေး	mjei:
granddaughter	မြေးမ	mjei: ma.
grandchildren	မြေးများ	mjei: mja:

uncle	ဦးလေး	u: lei:
aunt	အဒေါ်	ado
nephew	တူ	tu
niece	တူမ	tu ma.

mother-in-law (wife's mother)	ယောက္ခမ	jau' khama.
father-in-law (husband's father)	ယောက္ခထီး	jau' khadi:
son-in-law (daughter's husband)	သားမက်	tha: me'
stepmother	မိထွေး	mi. dwei:
stepfather	ပထွေး	pahtwei:

infant	နို့စို့ကလေး	nou. zou. galei:
baby (infant)	ကလေးငယ်	kalei: nge
little boy, kid	ကလေး	kalei:

| wife | မိန်းမ | mein: ma. |
| husband | ယောက်ျား | jau' kja: |

| spouse (husband) | ခင်ပွန်း | khin bun: |
| spouse (wife) | ဇနီး | zani: |

married (masc.)	မိန်းမရှိသော	mein: ma. shi. de.
married (fem.)	ယောက်ျားရှိသော	jau' kja: shi de
single (unmarried)	လူလွတ်ဖြစ်သော	lu lu' hpji te.
bachelor	လူပျို	lu bjou
divorced (masc.)	တစ်ခုလပ်ဖြစ်သော	ti' khu. la' hpji' te.

| widow | မုဆိုးမ | mu. zou: ma. |
| widower | မုဆိုးဖို | mu. zou: bou |

| relative | ဆွေမျိုး | hswe mjou: |
| close relative | ဆွေမျိုးရင်းချာ | hswe mjou: jin: gja |

| distant relative | ဆွေမျိုးနီးစပ် | hswe mjou: ni: za' |
| relatives | မွေးချင်းများ | mwei: chin: mja: |

orphan (boy or girl)	မိဘမဲ့	mi. ba me.
orphan (boy)	မိဘမဲ့ကလေး	mi. ba me. ga lei:
orphan (girl)	မိဘမဲ့ကလေးမ	mi. ba me. ga lei: ma
guardian (of a minor)	အုပ်ထိန်းသူ	ou' htin: dhu
to adopt (a boy)	သားအဖြစ်မွေးစားသည်	tha: ahpji' mwei: za: de
to adopt (a girl)	သမီးအဖြစ်မွေးစားသည်	thami: ahpji' mwei: za: de

60. Friends. Coworkers

friend (masc.)	သူငယ်ချင်း	thu nge gjin:
friend (fem.)	မိန်းကလေးသူငယ်ချင်း	mein: galei: dhu nge gjin:
friendship	ခင်မင်ရင်းနှီးမှု	khin min jin: ni: hmu,
to be friends	ခင်မင်သည်	khin min de
buddy (masc.)	အပေါင်းအသင်း	apaun: athin:
buddy (fem.)	အပေါင်းအသင်း	apaun: athin:
partner	လုပ်ဖော်ကိုင်ဖက်	lou' hpo kain be'
chief (boss)	အကြီးအကဲ	akji: ake:
superior (n)	အထက်လူကြီး	a hte' lu gji:
owner, proprietor	ပိုင်ရှင်	pain shin
subordinate (n)	လက်အောက်ခံအမှုထမ်း	le' au' khan ahmu. htan:
colleague	လုပ်ဖော်ကိုင်ဖက်	lou' hpo kain be'
acquaintance (person)	အကျွမ်းဝင်မှု	akjwan: win hmu.
fellow traveler	ခရီးဖော်	khaji: bo
classmate	တစ်တန်းတည်းသား	ti' tan: de: dha:
neighbor (masc.)	အိမ်နီးနားချင်း	ein ni: na: gjin:
neighbor (fem.)	မိန်းကွလေးအိမ်နီး နားချင်း	mein: galei: ein: ni: na: gjin:
neighbors	အိမ်နီးနားချင်းများ	ein ni: na: gjin: mja:

HUMAN BODY. MEDICINE

61. Head

head	ခေါင်း	gaun:
face	မျက်နှာ	mje' hna
nose	နှာခေါင်း	hna gaun:
mouth	ပါးစပ်	pa: zi'
eye	မျက်စိ	mje' si.
eyes	မျက်စိများ	mje' si. mja:
pupil	သူငယ်အိမ်	thu nge ein
eyebrow	မျက်ခုံး	mje' khoun:
eyelash	မျက်တောင်	mje' taun
eyelid	မျက်ခွံ	mje' khwan
tongue	လျာ	sha
tooth	သွား	thwa:
lips	နှတ်ခမ်း	hna' khan:
cheekbones	ပါးရိုး	pa: jou:
gum	သွားဖုံး	thwahpoun:
palate	အာခေါင်	a gaun
nostrils	နှာခေါင်းပေါက်	hna gaun: bau'
chin	မေးစေ့	mei: zei.
jaw	မေးရိုး	mei: jou:
cheek	ပါး	pa:
forehead	နဖူး	na. hpu:
temple	နားထင်	na: din
ear	နားရွက်	na: jwe'
back of the head	နောက်စေ့	nau' sei.
neck	လည်ပင်း	le bin:
throat	လည်ချောင်း	le gjaun:
hair	ဆံပင်	zabin
hairstyle	ဆံပင်ပုံစံ	zabin boun zan
haircut	ဆံပင်ညှပ်သည့်ပုံစံ	zabin hnja' thi. boun zan
wig	ဆံပင်တု	zabin du.
mustache	နှတ်ခမ်းမွေး	hnou' khan: hmwei:
beard	မုတ်ဆိတ်မွေး	mou' hsei' hmwei:
to have (a beard, etc.)	အရှည်ထားသည်	ashei hta' de
braid	ကျစ်ဆံမြီး	kji' zan mji:
sideburns	ပါးသိုင်းမွေး	pa: dhain: hmwei:
red-haired (adj)	ဆံပင်အနီရောင်ရှိသော	zabin ani jaun shi. de

gray (hair)	အရောင်ဖျော့သော	ajaun bjo. de.
bald (adj)	ထိပ်ခေါင်းပြောင်သော	htei' pjaun de.
bald patch	ဆံပင်ကျွတ်နေသောနေရာ	zabin kju' nei dho nei ja
ponytail	မြင်းမြီးပုံဆံပင်	mjin: mji: boun zan zan bin
bangs	ဆံရစ်	hsaji'

62. Human body

hand	လက်	le'
arm	လက်မောင်း	le' maun:
finger	လက်ချောင်း	le' chaun:
toe	ခြေချောင်း	chei gjaun:
thumb	လက်မ	le' ma
little finger	လက်သန်း	le' than:
nail	လက်သည်းခွံ	le' the: dou' tan zin:
fist	လက်သီး	le' thi:
palm	လက်ဝါး	le' wa:
wrist	လက်ကောက်ဝတ်	le' kau' wa'
forearm	လက်ဖျံ	le' hpjan
elbow	တံတောင်ဆစ်	daduan zi'
shoulder	ပခုံး	pakhoun:
leg	ခြေထောက်	chei htau'
foot	ခြေထောက်	chei htau'
knee	ဒူး	du:
calf (part of leg)	ခြေသလုံးကြွက်သား	chei dha. loun: gjwe' dha:
hip	တင်ပါး	tin ba:
heel	ခြေဖနောင့်	chei ba. naun.
body	ခန္ဓာကိုယ်	khan da kou
stomach	ဗိုက်	bai'
chest	ရင်ဘတ်	jin ba'
breast	နို့	nou.
flank	နံပါး	nan ba:
back	ကျော	kjo:
lower back	ခါးအောက်ပိုင်း	kha: au' pain:
waist	ခါး	kha:
navel (belly button)	ချက်	che'
buttocks	တင်ပါး	tin ba:
bottom	နောက်ပိုင်း	nau' pain:
beauty mark	မဲ့	hme.
birthmark (café au lait spot)	မွေးရာပါအမှတ်	mwei: ja ba ahma'
tattoo	တက်တူး	te' tu:
scar	အမာရွတ်	ama ju'

63. Diseases

sickness	ရောဂါ	jo: ga
to be sick	ဖျားနာသည်	hpa: na de
health	ကျန်းမာရေး	kjan: ma jei:
runny nose (coryza)	နာစေးခြင်း	hna zei: gjin:
tonsillitis	အာသီးရောင်ခြင်း	a sha. jaun gjin:
cold (illness)	အအေးမိခြင်း	aei: mi. gjin:
to catch a cold	အအေးမိသည်	aei: mi. de
bronchitis	ချောင်းဆိုးရင်ကျပ်နာ	gaun: ou: jin gja' na
pneumonia	အဆုတ်ရောင်ရောဂါ	ahsou' jaun jo: ga
flu, influenza	တုပ်ကွေး	tou' kwei:
nearsighted (adj)	အဝေးမှုန်သော	awei: hmun de.
farsighted (adj)	အနီးမှုန်	ani: hmoun
strabismus (crossed eyes)	မျက်စိစွေခြင်း	mje' zi. zwei gjin:
cross-eyed (adj)	မျက်စိစွေသော	mje' zi. zwei de.
cataract	နာမကျန်းဖြစ်ခြင်း	na. ma. gjan: bji' chin:
glaucoma	ရေတိမ်	jei dein
stroke	လေသင်တုန်းဖြတ်ခြင်း	lei dhin doun: bja' chin:
heart attack	နှလုံးဖောက်ပြန်မှု	hnaloun: bau' bjan hmu.
myocardial infarction	နှလုံးကြွက်သား ပိုင်ခြင်း	hnaloun: gjwe' tha: bou' chin:
paralysis	သွက်ချာပါဒ	thwe' cha ba da.
to paralyze (vt)	ဆိုင်းတွသွားသည်	hsain: dwa dhwa: de
allergy	မတည့်ခြင်း	ma. de. gjin:
asthma	ပန်းနာ	pan: na
diabetes	ဆီးချိုရောဂါ	hsi: gjou jau ba
toothache	သွားကိုက်ခြင်း	thwa: kai' chin:
caries	သွာပိုးစားခြင်း	thwa: pou: za: gjin:
diarrhea	ဝမ်းလျှောခြင်း	wan: sho: gjin:
constipation	ဝမ်းချုပ်ခြင်း	wan: gjou' chin:
stomach upset	ဗိုက်နာခြင်း	bai' na gjin:
food poisoning	အစာအဆိပ်သင့်ခြင်း	asa: ahsei' thin. gjin:
to get food poisoning	အစားမှားခြင်း	asa: hma: gjin:
arthritis	အဆစ်ရောင်နာ	ahsi' jaun na
rickets	အရိုးပျော့နာ	ajou: bjau. na
rheumatism	ဒုလာ	du la
atherosclerosis	နှလုံးသွေးကြော အဆီပိတ်ခြင်း	hna. loun: twei: kjau ahsi pei' khin:
gastritis	အစာအိမ်ရောင်ရမ်းနာ	asa: ein jaun jan: na
appendicitis	အူအတက်ရောင်ခြင်း	au hte' jaun gjin:
cholecystitis	သည်းခြေပြွန်ရောင်ခြင်း	thi: gjei bjun jaun gjin:

ulcer	ဖက်ခွက်နာ	hpe' khwe' na
measles	ဝက်သက်	we' the'
rubella (German measles)	ဂျုက်သိုး	gjou' thou:
jaundice	အသားဝါရောဂါ	atha: wa jo: ga
hepatitis	အသည်းရောင်ရောဂါ	athe: jaun jau ba
schizophrenia	စိတ်ကစဉ့်ကလျားရောဂါ	sei' ga. zin. ga. lja: jo: ga
rabies (hydrophobia)	ခွေးရူးပြန်ရောဂါ	khwei: ju: bjan jo: ba
neurosis	စိတ်မှမမှန်ခြင်း	sei' mu ma. hman gjin:
concussion	ဦးနှောက်ထိခိုက်ခြင်း	oun: hnau' hti. gai' chin:
cancer	ကင်ဆာ	kin hsa
sclerosis	အသားမှုင်ခက် မာသွားခြင်း	atha: hmjin kha' ma dwa: gjin:
multiple sclerosis	အာရုံကြောပျက်စီး ရောင်ရမ်းသည့်ရောဂါ	a joun gjo: bje' si: jaun jan: dhi. jo: ga
alcoholism	အရက်နာစွဲခြင်း	aje' na zwe: gjin:
alcoholic (n)	အရက်သမား	aje' dha. ma:
syphilis	ဆစ်ဖလစ်ကာလ သားရောဂါ	his' hpa. li' ka la. dha: jo: ba
AIDS	ကိုယ်ခံအားကျကူး စက်ရောဂါ	kou khan a: kja ku: za' jau ba
tumor	အသားပို	atha: pou
malignant (adj)	ကင်ဆာဖြစ်နေသော	kin hsa bji' nei de.
benign (adj)	ပြန့်ပွားခြင်း မရှိသော	pjan. bwa: gjin: ma. shi. de.
fever	အဖျားတက်ရောဂါ	ahpja: de' jo: ga
malaria	ငှက်ဖျားရောဂါ	hnge' hpja: jo: ba
gangrene	ဂန်ဂရိန်ားရောဂါ	gan ga. ji na jo: ba
seasickness	လှိုင်းမူးခြင်း	hlain: mu: gjin:
epilepsy	ဝက်ရူးပြန်ရောဂါ	we' ju: bjan jo: ga
epidemic	ကပ်ရောဂါ	ka' jo ba
typhus	တိုက်ဖိုက်ရောဂါ	tai' hpai' jo: ba
tuberculosis	တီဘီရောဂါ	ti bi jo: ba
cholera	ကာလဝမ်းရောဂါ	ka la. wan: jau ga
plague (bubonic ~)	ကပ်ဆိုး	ka' hsou:

64. Symptoms. Treatments. Part 1

symptom	လက္ခဏာ	le' khana
temperature	အပူချိန်	apu gjein
high temperature (fever)	ကိုယ်အပူချိန်တက်	kou apu chain de'
pulse (heartbeat)	သွေးခုန်နှုန်း	thwei: khoun hnan:
dizziness (vertigo)	မူးနှောက်ခြင်း	mu: nau' chin:
hot (adj)	ပူသော	pu dho:

shivering	တုန်ခြင်း	toun gjin:
pale (e.g., ~ face)	ဖြူရော်သော	hpju jo de.
cough	ချောင်းဆိုးခြင်း	gaun: zou: gjin:
to cough (vi)	ချောင်းဆိုးသည်	gaun: zou: de
to sneeze (vi)	နာချေသည်	hna gjei de
faint	အားနည်းခြင်း	a: ne: gjin:
to faint (vi)	သတိလစ်သည်	dhadi. li' te
bruise (hématome)	ပွန်းပဲ့ဒက်ရာ	pun: be. dan ja
bump (lump)	ဆောင့်မိခြင်း	hsaun. mi. gjin:
to bang (bump)	ဆောင့်မိသည်	hsaun. mi. de.
contusion (bruise)	ပွန်းပဲ့ဒက်ရာ	pun: be. dan ja
to get a bruise	ပွန်းပဲ့ဒက်ရာရသည်	pun: be. dan ja ja. de
to limp (vi)	ထော့နဲ့ထော့နဲ့လျှောက်သည်	hto. ne. hto. ne. shau' te
dislocation	အဆစ်လွဲခြင်း	ahsi' lwe: gjin:
to dislocate (vt)	အဆစ်လွဲသည်	ahsi' lwe: de
fracture	ကျိုးအက်ခြင်း	kjou: e' chin:
to have a fracture	ကျိုးအက်သည်	kjou: e' te
cut (e.g., paper ~)	ရှသည်	sha. de
to cut oneself	ရှမိသည်	sha. mi. de
bleeding	သွေးထွက်ခြင်း	thwei: htwe' chin:
burn (injury)	မီးလောင်သည့်ဒက်ရာ	mi: laun de. dan ja
to get burned	မီးလောင်ဒက်ရာရသည်	mi: laun dan ja ja. de
to prick (vt)	ဖောက်သည်	hpau' te
to prick oneself	ကိုယ်တိုင်ဖောက်သည်	kou tain hpau' te
to injure (vt)	ထိခိုက်ဒက်ရာရသည်	hti. gai' dan ja ja. de
injury	ထိခိုက်ဒက်ရာ	hti. gai' dan ja
wound	ဒက်ရာ	dan ja
trauma	စိတ်ဒက်ရာ	sei' dan ja
to be delirious	ကယောင်ကတမ်းဖြစ်သည်	kajaun ka dan: bi' te
to stutter (vi)	တုံ့နေ့းတုံ့	toun. hnei: toun.
	နေ့းဖြစ်သည်	hnei: bji' te
sunstroke	အပူလျှပ်ခြင်း	apu hlja' chin

65. Symptoms. Treatments. Part 2

pain, ache	နာကျင်မှု	na gjin hmu.
splinter (in foot, etc.)	ပိုထွက်သောအစ	pe. dwe' tho: asa.
sweat (perspiration)	ချွေး	chwei:
to sweat (perspire)	ချွေးထွက်သည်	chwei: htwe' te
vomiting	အန်ခြင်း	an gjin:
convulsions	အကြောလိုက်ခြင်း	akjo: lai' chin:
pregnant (adj)	ကိုယ်ဝန်ဆောင်ထားသော	kou wun hsaun da: de.

to be born	မွေးဖွားသည်	mwei: bwa: de
delivery, labor	မီးဖွားခြင်း	mi: bwa: gjin:
to deliver (~ a baby)	မီးဖွားသည်	mi: bwa: de
abortion	ကိုယ်ဝန်ဖျက်ချခြင်း	kou wun hpje' cha chin:
breathing, respiration	အသက်ရှူခြင်း	athe' shu gjin:
in-breath (inhalation)	ဝင်လေ	win lei
out-breath (exhalation)	ထွက်လေ	htwe' lei
to exhale (breathe out)	အသက်ရှူထုတ်သည်	athe' shu dou' te
to inhale (vi)	အသက်ရှူသွင်းသည်	athe' shu dhwin: de
disabled person	ကိုယ်အင်္ဂါမသန်စွမ်းသူ	kou an ga ma. dhan swan: dhu
cripple	မသန်မစွမ်းသူ	ma. dhan ma. zwan dhu
drug addict	ဆေးစွဲသူ	hsei: zwe: dhu
deaf (adj)	နားမကြားသော	na: ma. gja: de.
mute (adj)	ဆွံ့အသော	hsun. ade.
deaf mute (adj)	ဆွံ့အ နားမကြားသူ	hsun. ana: ma. gja: dhu
mad, insane (adj)	စိတ်မနှံ့သော	sei' ma. hnan. de.
madman (demented person)	စိတ်မနှံ့သူ	sei' ma. hnan. dhu
madwoman	စိတ်ဝေဒနာရှင်မိန်းကလေး	sei' wei da. na shin mein: ga. lei:
to go insane	ရူးသွပ်သည်	ju: dhu' de
gene	မျိုးရိုးဗီဇ	mjou: jou: bi za.
immunity	ကိုယ်ခံအား	kou gan a:
hereditary (adj)	မျိုးရိုးလိုက်သော	mjou: jou: lou' te.
congenital (adj)	မွေးရာပါဖြစ်သော	mwei: ja ba bji' te.
virus	ဗိုင်းရပ်ပိုးမွှား	bain: ja' pou: hmwa:
microbe	အဏုဇီဝရုပ်	anu zi wa. jou'
bacterium	ဗက်တီးရီးယားပိုး	be' ti: ji: ja: bou:
infection	ရောဂါကူးစက်မှု	jo ga gu: ze' hmu.

66. Symptoms. Treatments. Part 3

hospital	ဆေးရုံ	hsei: joun
patient	လူနာ	lu na
diagnosis	ရောဂါစစ်ဆေးခြင်း	jo ga zi' hsei: gjin:
cure	ဆေးကုထုံး	hsei: ku. doun:
medical treatment	ဆေးဝါးကုသမှု	hsei: wa: gu. dha. hmu.
to get treatment	ဆေးကုသမှုခံယူသည်	hsei: ku. dha. hmu. dha de
to treat (~ a patient)	ပြုစုသည်	pju. zu. de
to nurse (look after)	ပြုစုစောင့်ရှောက်သည်	pju. zu. zaun. shau' te
care (nursing ~)	ပြုစုစောင့်ရှောက်ခြင်း	pju. zu. zaun. shau' chin:
operation, surgery	ခွဲစိတ်ကုသခြင်း	khwe: zei' ku. dha. hin:

to bandage (head, limb)	ပတ်တီးစည်းသည်	pa' ti: ze: de
bandaging	ပတ်တီးစည်းခြင်း	pa' ti: ze: gjin:
vaccination	ကာကွယ်ဆေးထိုးခြင်း	ka gwe hsei: dou: gjin:
to vaccinate (vt)	ကာကွယ်ဆေးထိုးသည်	ka gwe hsei: dou: de
injection, shot	ဆေးထိုးခြင်း	hsei: dou: gjin:
to give an injection	ဆေးထိုးသည်	hsei: dou: de
attack	ရောဂါ ရှုတ်တွရက်ကျရောက်ခြင်း	jo ga jou' ta. je' kja. jau' chin:
amputation	ဖြတ်တောက်ကုသခြင်း	hpja' tau' ku. dha gjin:
to amputate (vt)	ဖြတ်တောက်ကုသသည်	hpja' tau' ku. dha de
coma	မေ့မြောခြင်း	mei. mjo: gjin:
to be in a coma	မေ့မြောသည်	mei. mjo: de
intensive care	အစွမ်းကုန်ပြုစုခြင်း	aswan: boun bju. zu. bjin:
to recover (~ from flu)	ရောဂါသက်သာလာသည်	jo ga dhe' tha la de
condition (patient's ~)	ကျန်းမာရေးအခြေအနေ	kjan: ma jei: achei a nei
consciousness	ပြန်လည်သတိရလာခြင်း	pjan le dhadi. ja. la. gjin:
memory (faculty)	မှတ်ဉာဏ်	hma' njan
to pull out (tooth)	နုတ်သည်	hna' te
filling	သွားပေါက်ဖာထေးမှု	thwa: bau' hpa dei: hmu.
to fill (a tooth)	ဖာသည်	hpa de
hypnosis	အိပ်မွေ့ရှုခြင်း	ei' mwei. gja. gjin:
to hypnotize (vt)	အိပ်မွေ့ရှုသည်	ei' mwei. gja. de

67. Medicine. Drugs. Accessories

medicine, drug	ဆေးဝါး	hsei: wa:
remedy	ကုသခြင်း	ku. dha. gjin:
to prescribe (vt)	ဆေးအညွှန်းပေးသည်	hsa: ahnjun: bwe: de
prescription	ဆေးညွှန်း	hsei: hnjun:
tablet, pill	ဆေးပြား	hsei: bja:
ointment	လိမ်းဆေး	lein: zei:
ampule	လေလုံဖန်ပုလင်းငယ်	lei loun ban bu. lin: nge
mixture, solution	စပ်ဆေးရည်	sa' ei: je
syrup	ဖျော်ရည်ဆီ	hpjo jei zi
capsule	ဆေးတောင့်	hsei: daun.
powder	အမှုန့်	ahmoun.
gauze bandage	ပတ်တီး	pa' ti:
cotton wool	ဝွန်းလိပ်	gwan: lei'
iodine	တင်ဂျာအိုင်ဒင်း	tin gja ein din:
Band-Aid	ပလာစတာ	pa. la sata
eyedropper	မျက်စဉ်းခတ်ကိရိယာ	mje' zin: ba' ki. ji. ja
thermometer	အပူချိန်တိုင်းကိရိယာ	apu gjein dain: gi. ji. ja

syringe	ဆေးထိုးပြွတ်	hsei: dou: bju'
wheelchair	ဘီးတပ်ကုလားထိုင်	bi: da' ku. la: dain
crutches	ချိုင်းထောက်	chain: dau'

painkiller	အကိုက်အခဲပျောက်ဆေး	akai' akhe: pjau' hsei:
laxative	ဝမ်းနုတ်ဆေး	wan: hnou' hsei:
spirits (ethanol)	အရက်ပြန်	aje' pjan
medicinal herbs	ဆေးဖက်ဝင်အပင်များ	hsei: hpa' win apin mja:
herbal (~ tea)	ဆေးဖက်ဝင်အပင် နှင့်ဆိုင်သော	hsei: hpa' win apin hnin. zain de.

APARTMENT

apartment	တိုက်ခန်း	tai' khan:
room	အခန်း	akhan:
bedroom	အိပ်ခန်း	ei' khan:
dining room	ထမင်းစားခန်း	htamin: za: gan:
living room	ဧည့်ခန်း	e. gan:
study (home office)	အိမ်တွင်းရုံးခန်းလေး	ein dwin: joun: gan: lei:
entry room	ဝင်ပေါက်	win bau'
bathroom (room with a bath or shower)	ရေချိုးခန်း	jei gjou gan:
half bath	အိမ်သာ	ein dha
ceiling	မျက်နှာကြက်	mje' hna gje'
floor	ကြမ်းပြင်	kan: pjin
corner	ထောင့်	htaun.

furniture	ပရိဘောဂ	pa ri. bo: ga.
table	စားပွဲ	sa: bwe:
chair	ကုလားထိုင်	kala; dain
bed	ကုတင်	ku din
couch, sofa	ဆိုဖာ	hsou hpa
armchair	လက်တင်ပါသောကုလားထိုင်	le' tin ba dho: ku. la: dain
bookcase	စာအုပ်စင်	sa ou' sin
shelf	စင်	sin
wardrobe	ဒီရို	bi jou
coat rack (wall-mounted ~)	နံရံကပ်အဝတ်ချိတ်စင်	nan jan ga' awu' gei' zin
coat stand	အဝတ်ချိတ်စင်	awu' gjei' sin
bureau, dresser	အံဆွဲပါ မှန်တင်ခုံ	an. zwe: pa hman din khoun
coffee table	စားပွဲပု	sa: bwe: bu.
mirror	မှန်	hman
carpet	ကော်ဇော	ko zo:
rug, small carpet	ကော်ဇော	ko zo:
fireplace	မီးလင်းဖို	mi: lin: bou

candle	ဖယောင်းတိုင်	hpa. jaun dain
candlestick	ဖယောင်းတိုင်စိုက်သောတိုင်	hpa. jaun dain zou' tho dain
drapes	ခန်းဆီးရည်	khan: zi: shei
wallpaper	နံရံကပ်စက္ကူ	nan jan ga' se' ku
blinds (jalousie)	ယင်းလိပ်	jin: lei'
table lamp	စားပွဲတင်မီးအိမ်	sa: bwe: din mi: ein
wall lamp (sconce)	နံရံကပ်မီး	nan jan ga' mi:
floor lamp	မတ်တပ်မီးစခလောင်း	ma' ta' mi: za. laun:
chandelier	မီးပန်းဆိုင်း	mi: ban: zain:
leg (of chair, table)	ခြေထောက်	chei htau'
armrest	လက်တန်း	le' tan:
back (backrest)	နောက်မှီ	nau' mi
drawer	အံဆွဲ	an. zwe:

70. Bedding

bedclothes	အိပ်ရာခင်းများ	ei' ja khin: mja:
pillow	ခေါင်းအုံး	gaun: oun:
pillowcase	ခေါင်းစွပ်	gaun: zu'
duvet, comforter	စောင်	saun
sheet	အိပ်ရာခင်း	ei' ja khin:
bedspread	အိပ်ရာဖုံး	ei' ja hpoun:

71. Kitchen

kitchen	မီးဖိုခန်း	mi: bou gan:
gas	ဓာတ်ငွေ့	da' ngwei.
gas stove (range)	ဂတ်စ်မီးဖို	ga' s mi: bou
electric stove	လျပ်စစ်မီးဖို	hlja' si' si: bou
oven	မုန့်ဖုတ်ရန်ဖို	moun. bou' jan bou
microwave oven	မိုက်ခရိုဝေ့ဗ်	mou' kha. jou wei. b
refrigerator	ရေခဲသေတ္တာ	je ge: dhi' ta
freezer	ရေခဲခန်း	jei ge: gan:
dishwasher	ပန်းကန်ဆေးစက်	bagan: zei: ze'
meat grinder	အသားကြိတ်စက်	atha: kjei' za'
juicer	အသီးဖျော်စက်	athi: hpjo ze'
toaster	ပေါင်မုန့်ကင်စက်	paun moun. gin ze'
mixer	မွှေစက်	hmwei ze'
coffee machine	ကော်ဖီဖျော်စက်	ko hpi hpjo ze'
coffee pot	ကော်ဖီအိုး	ko hpi ou:
coffee grinder	ကော်ဖီကြိတ်စက်	ko hpi kjei ze'

kettle	ရေနွေးကရားအိုး	jei nwei: gaja: ou:
teapot	လက်ဘက်ရည်အိုး	le' be' ji ou:
lid	အိုးအဖုံး	ou: ahpoun:
tea strainer	လက်ဖက်ရည်စစ်	le' hpe' ji zi'

spoon	ဇွန်း	zun:
teaspoon	လက်ဖက်ရည်ဇွန်း	le' hpe' ji zwan:
soup spoon	အရည်သောက်ဇွန်း	aja: dhau' zun:
fork	ခက်ရင်း	khajin:
knife	ဓား	da:

tableware (dishes)	အိုးခွက်ပန်းကန်	ou: kwe' pan: gan
plate (dinner ~)	ပန်းကန်ပြား	bagan: bja:
saucer	အောက်ခံပန်းကန်ပြား	au' khan ban: kan pja:

shot glass	ဖန်ခွက်	hpan gwe'
glass (tumbler)	ဖန်ခွက်	hpan gwe'
cup	ခွက်	khwe'

sugar bowl	သကြားခွက်	dhagja: khwe'
salt shaker	ဆားဘူး	hsa: bu:
pepper shaker	ငြုတ်ကောင်းဘူး	njou' kaun: bu:
butter dish	ထောပတ်ခွက်	hto: ba' khwe'

stock pot (soup pot)	ပေါင်းအိုး	paun: ou:
frying pan (skillet)	ဟင်းကြော်အိုး	hin: gjo ou:
ladle	ဟင်းခပ်ဇွန်း	hin: ga' zun
colander	ဆန်ခါ	zaga
tray (serving ~)	လင်ပန်း	lin ban:

bottle	ပုလင်း	palin:
jar (glass)	ဖန်ဘူး	hpan bu:
can	သံဘူး	than bu:

bottle opener	ပုလင်းဖောက်တံ	pu. lin: bau' tan
can opener	သံဘူးဖောက်တံ	than bu: bau' tan
corkscrew	ဝက်အူဖောက်တံ	we' u bau' dan
filter	ရေစစ်	jei zi'
to filter (vt)	စစ်သည်	si' te

| trash, garbage (food waste, etc.) | အမှိုက် | ahmai' |
| trash can (kitchen ~) | အမှိုက်ပုံး | ahmai' poun: |

72. Bathroom

bathroom	ရေချိုးခန်း	jei gjou gan:
water	ရေ	jei
faucet	ရေပိုက်ခေါင်း	jei bai' khaun:
hot water	ရေပူ	jei bu

cold water	ရေအေး	jei ei:
toothpaste	သွားတိုက်ဆေး	thwa: tai' hsei:
to brush one's teeth	သွားတိုက်သည်	thwa: tai' te
toothbrush	သွားတိုက်တံ	thwa: tai' tan
to shave (vi)	ရိတ်သည်	jei' te
shaving foam	မုတ်ဆိတ်တွေ့ရိတ်သုံး	mou' hsei' jei' thoun:
	ဆပ်ပြာမြှုပ်	za' pja hmjou'
razor	သင်တုန်းဓား	thin toun: da:
to wash (one's hands, etc.)	ဆေးသည်	hsei: de
to take a bath	ရေချိုးသည်	jei gjou: de
shower	ရေပန်း	jei ban:
to take a shower	ရေချိုးသည်	jei gjou: de
bathtub	ရေချိုးကန်	jei gjou: gan
toilet (toilet bowl)	အိမ်သာ	ein dha
sink (washbasin)	လက်ဆေးကန်	le' hsei: kan
soap	ဆပ်ပြာ	hsa' pja
soap dish	ဆပ်ပြာခွက်	hsa' pja gwe'
sponge	ရေမြှုပ်	jei hmjou'
shampoo	ခေါင်းလျှော်ရည်	gaun: sho je
towel	တဘက်	tabe'
bathrobe	ရေချိုးခန်းဝတ်စုံ	jei gjou: gan: wu' soun
laundry (laundering)	အဝတ်လျှော်ခြင်း	awu' sho gjin
washing machine	အဝတ်လျှော်စက်	awu' sho ze'
to do the laundry	ဒီဘီလျှော်သည်	dou bi jo de
laundry detergent	အဝတ်လျှော်ဆပ်ပြာမှုန့်.	awu' sho hsa' pja hmun.

73. Household appliances

TV set	ရုပ်မြင်သံကြားစက်	jou' mjin dhan gja: ze'
tape recorder	အသံသွင်းစက်	athan dhwin: za'
VCR (video recorder)	ဗီဒီယိုပြစက်	bi di jou bja. ze'
radio	ရေဒီယို	rei di jou
player (CD, MP3, etc.)	ပလေယာစက်	pa. lei ja ze'
video projector	ဗီဒီယိုပရိုဂျက်တာ	bi di jou pa. jou gje' da
home movie theater	အိမ်တွင်းရုပ်ရှင်ခန်း	ein dwin: jou' shin gan:
DVD player	ဒီဗီဒီပလေယာ	di bi di ba lei ja
amplifier	အသံချဲ့စက်	athan che. zek
video game console	ဂိမ်းခလုတ်	gein: kha lou'
video camera	ဗွီဒီယိုကင်မရာ	bwi di jou kin ma. ja
camera (photo)	ကင်မရာ	kin ma. ja
digital camera	ဒီဂျစ်တယ်ကင်မရာ	digji' te gin ma. ja
vacuum cleaner	ဖုန်စုပ်စက်	hpoun zou' se'

iron (e.g., steam ~)	မီးပူ	mi: bu
ironing board	မီးပူတိုက်ရန်စင်	mi: bu tai' jan zin
telephone	တယ်လီဖုန်း	te li hpoun:
cell phone	မိုဘိုင်းဖုန်း	mou bain: hpoun:
typewriter	လက်နှိပ်စက်	le' hnei' se'
sewing machine	အပ်ချုပ်စက်	a' chou' se'
microphone	စကားပြောခွက်	zaga: bjo: gwe'
headphones	နားကြပ်	na: kja'
remote control (TV)	အဝေးထိန်းကိရိယာ	awei: htin: ki. ja. ja
CD, compact disc	စီဒီပြား	si di bja:
cassette, tape	တိပ်ခွေ	tei' khwei
vinyl record	ရှေးခေတ်သုံးဓာတ်ပြား	shei: gi' thoun da' pja:

THE EARTH. WEATHER

74. Outer space

space	အာကာသ	akatha.
space (as adj)	အာကာသနှင့်ဆိုင်သော	akatha. hnin zain dho:
outer space	အာကာသဟင်းလင်းပြင်	akatha. hin: lin: bjin
world	ကမ္ဘာ	ga ba
universe	စကြာဝဠာ	sa kja wa. la
galaxy	ကြယ်စုတန်း	kje zu. dan:
star	ကြယ်	kje
constellation	ကြယ်နက္ခတ်စု	kje ne' kha' zu.
planet	ဂြိုဟ်	gjou
satellite	ဂြိုဟ်ငယ်	gjou nge
meteorite	ဥက္ကာခဲ	ou' ka ge:
comet	ကြယ်တံခွန်	kje dagun
asteroid	ဂြိုဟ်သိမ်ဂြိုဟ်မွှား	gjou dhein gjou hmwa:
orbit	ပတ်လမ်း	pa' lan:
to revolve	လည်သည်	le de
(~ around the Earth)		
atmosphere	လေထု	lei du.
the Sun	နေ	nei
solar system	နေစကြာဝဠာ	nei ze kja. wala
solar eclipse	နေကြတ်ခြင်း	nei gja' chin:
the Earth	ကမ္ဘာလုံး	ga ba loun:
the Moon	လ	la.
Mars	အင်္ဂါဂြိုဟ်	in ga gjou
Venus	သောကြာဂြိုဟ်	thau' kja gjou'
Jupiter	ကြာသပတေးဂြိုဟ်	kja dha ba. dei: gjou'
Saturn	စနေဂြိုဟ်	sanei gjou'
Mercury	ဗုဒ္ဓဟူးဂြိုဟ်	bou' da. gjou'
Uranus	ယူရေးနက်ဂြိုဟ်	ju rei: na' gjou
Neptune	နက်ပကျွန်းဂြိုဟ်	ne' pa. gjun: gjou
Pluto	ပလူတိုဂြိုဟ်	pa lu tou gjou '
Milky Way	နဂါးငွေ့ကြယ်စုတန်း	na. ga: ngwe. gje zu dan:
Great Bear (Ursa Major)	မြှောက်ပိုင်းဝက်ရှင်	mjau' pain: gajei'
	ဘဲ့ကြယ်စု	be:j gje zu.

North Star	ဓူဝံကြယ်	du wan gje
Martian	အင်္ဂါဂြိုဟ်သား	in ga gjou dha:
extraterrestrial (n)	အခြားကမ္ဘာဂြိုဟ်သား	apja: ga ba gjou dha
alien	ဂြိုဟ်သား	gjou dha:
flying saucer	ပန်းကန်ပြားပျံ	bagan: bja: bjan
spaceship	အာကာသယာဉ်	akatha. jin
space station	အာကာသစခန်း	akatha. za khan:
blast-off	လွှတ်တင်ခြင်း	hlu' tin gjin:
engine	အင်ဂျင်	in gjin
nozzle	နော်ဇယ်	no ze
fuel	လောင်စာ	laun za
cockpit, flight deck	လေယာဉ်မောင်းအခန်း	lei jan maun akhan:
antenna	အင်တာနာတိုင်	in tan na tain
porthole	ပြတင်း	badin:
solar panel	နေရောင်ခြည်သုံးဘက်ထရီ	nei jaun gje dhoun: ba' hta ji
spacesuit	အာကာသဝတ်စုံ	akatha. wu' soun
weightlessness	အလေးချိန်ကင်းမဲ့ခြင်း	alei: gjein gin: me. gjin:
oxygen	အောက်ဆီဂျင်	au' hsi gjin
docking (in space)	အာကာသထဲချိတ်ဆက်ခြင်း	akatha. hte: chei' hse' chin:
to dock (vi, vt)	အာကာသထဲချိတ်ဆက်သည်	akatha. hte: chei' hse' te
observatory	နက္ခတ်မျှော်စင်	ne' kha' ta. mjo zin
telescope	အဝေးကြည့်မှန်ပြောင်း	awei: gji. hman bjaun:
to observe (vt)	လေ့လာကြည့်ရှုသည်	lei. la kji. hju. de
to explore (vt)	သုတေသနပြုသည်	thu. tei thana bjou de

75. The Earth

the Earth	ကမ္ဘာမြေကြီး	ga ba mjei kji:
the globe (the Earth)	ကမ္ဘာလုံး	ga ba loun:
planet	ဂြိုဟ်	gjou
atmosphere	လေထု	lei du.
geography	ပထဝီဝင်	pahtawi win
nature	သဘာဝ	tha. bawa
globe (table ~)	ကမ္ဘာလုံး	ga ba loun:
map	မြေပုံ	mjei boun
atlas	မြေပုံစာအုပ်	mjei boun za ou'
Europe	ဥရောပ	u. jo: pa
Asia	အာရှ	a sha.
Africa	အာဖရိက	apha. ri. ka.

Australia	သြစတြေးလျ	thja za djei: lja
America	အမေရိက	amei ji ka
North America	မြောက်အမေရိက	mjau' amei ri. ka.
South America	တောင်အမေရိက	taun amei ri. ka.

| Antarctica | အန္တာတိတ် | anta di' |
| the Arctic | အာတိတ် | a tei' |

76. Cardinal directions

north	မြောက်အရပ်	mjau' aja'
to the north	မြောက်ဘက်သို့	mjau' be' thou.
in the north	မြောက်ဘက်မှာ	mjau' be' hma
northern (adj)	မြောက်အရပ်နှင့်ဆိုင်သော	mjau' aja' hnin. zain de.

south	တောင်အရပ်	taun aja'
to the south	တောင်ဘက်သို့	taun be' thou.
in the south	တောင်ဘက်မှာ	taun be' hma
southern (adj)	တောင်အရပ်နှင့်ဆိုင်သော	taun aja' hnin. zain de.

west	အနောက်အရပ်	anau' aja'
to the west	အနောက်ဘက်သို့	anau' be' thou.
in the west	အနောက်ဘက်မှာ	anau' be' hma
western (adj)	အနောက်အရပ်နှင့်ဆိုင်သော	anau' aja' hnin. zain dho:

east	အရှေ့အရပ်	ashei. aja'
to the east	အရှေ့ဘက်သို့	ashei. be' hma
in the east	အရှေ့ဘက်မှာ	ashei. be' hma
eastern (adj)	အရှေ့အရပ်နှင့်ဆိုင်သော	ashei. aja' hnin. zain de.

77. Sea. Ocean

sea	ပင်လယ်	pin le
ocean	သမုဒ္ဒရာ	thamou' daja
gulf (bay)	ပင်လယ်ကွေ့	pin le gwe.
straits	ရေလက်ကြား	jei le' kja:

| land (solid ground) | ကုန်းမြေ | koun: mei |
| continent (mainland) | တိုက် | tai' |

island	ကျွန်း	kjun:
peninsula	ကျွန်းဆွယ်	kjun: zwe
archipelago	ကျွန်းစု	kjun: zu.

bay, cove	အော်	o
harbor	သင်္ဘောဆိပ်ကမ်း	thin: bo: zei' kan:
lagoon	ပင်လယ်ထုံးအိုင်	pin le doun: ain
cape	အငူ	angu

atoll	သန္တာကျောက်တန်းကျွန်းငယ်	than da gjau' tan: gjun: nge
reef	ကျောက်တန်း	kjau' tan:
coral	သန္တာကောင်	than da gaun
coral reef	သန္တာကျောက်တန်း	than da gjau' tan:
deep (adj)	နက်သော	ne' te.
depth (deep water)	အနက်	ane'
abyss	ချောက်နက်ကြီး	chau' ne' kji:
trench (e.g., Mariana ~)	မြောင်း	mjaun:
current (Ocean ~)	စီးကြောင်း	si: gaun:
to surround (bathe)	ဝိုင်းသည်	wain: de
shore	ကမ်းစပ်	kan: za'
coast	ကမ်းရေ	kan: gjei
flow (flood tide)	ရေတက်	jei de'
ebb (ebb tide)	ရေကျ	jei gja.
shoal	သောင်စွယ်	thaun zwe
bottom (~ of the sea)	ကြမ်းပြင်	kan: pjin
wave	လှိုင်း	hlain:
crest (~ of a wave)	လှိုင်းခေါင်းဖြူ	hlain: gaun: bju.
spume (sea foam)	အမြှုပ်	a hmjou'
storm (sea storm)	မုန်တိုင်း	moun dain:
hurricane	ဟာရီကိန်းမုန်တိုင်း	ha ji gain: moun dain:
tsunami	ဆူနာမိ	hsu na mi
calm (dead ~)	ရေသေ	jei dhei
quiet, calm (adj)	ငြိမ်သက်အေးဆေးသော	njein dhe' ei: zei: de.
pole	ဝင်ရိုးစွန်း	win jou: zun
polar (adj)	ဝင်ရိုးစွန်းနှင့်ဆိုင်သော	win jou: zun hnin. zain de.
latitude	လတ္တီတွဒ်	la' ti. tu'
longitude	လောင်ဂျီတွဒ်	laun gji twa'
parallel	လတ္တီတွဒ်မျဉ်း	la' ti. tu' mjin:
equator	အီကွေတာ	i kwei: da
sky	ကောင်းကင်	kaun: gin
horizon	မိုးကုပ်စက်ဝိုင်း	mou kou' se' wain:
air	လေထု	lei du.
lighthouse	မီးပြတိုက်	mi: bja dai'
to dive (vi)	ရေငုပ်သည်	jei ngou' te
to sink (ab. boat)	ရေမြုပ်သည်	jei mjou' te
treasures	ရတနာ	jadana

78. Seas' and Oceans' names

Atlantic Ocean	အတ္တလန္တိတ် သမုဒ္ဒရာ	a' ta. lan ti' thamou' daja
Indian Ocean	အိန္ဒိယ သမုဒ္ဒရာ	indi. ja thamou. daja
Pacific Ocean	ပစိဖိတ် သမုဒ္ဒရာ	pa. si. hpi' thamou' daja
Arctic Ocean	အာတိတ် သမုဒ္ဒရာ	a tei' thamou' daja
Black Sea	ပင်လယ်နက်	pin le ne'
Red Sea	ပင်လယ်နီ	pin le ni
Yellow Sea	ပင်လယ်ဝါ	pin le wa
White Sea	ပင်လယ်ဖြူ	pin le bju
Caspian Sea	ကက်စပီယန် ပင်လယ်	ke' za. pi jan pin le
Dead Sea	ပင်လယ်သေ	pin le dhe:
Mediterranean Sea	မြေထဲပင်လယ်	mjei hte: bin le
Aegean Sea	အေဂီယန်းပင်လယ်	ei gi jan: bin le
Adriatic Sea	အဒရီရာတစ်ပင်လယ်	a da yi ya ti' pin le
Arabian Sea	အာရေဘီးယန်း ပင်လယ်	a ra bi: an: bin le
Sea of Japan	ဂျပန် ပင်လယ်	gja pan pin le
Bering Sea	ဘယ်ရင်း ပင်လယ်	be jin: bin le
South China Sea	တောင်တရုတ်ပင်လယ်	taun dajou' pinle
Coral Sea	ကော်ရယ်လ်ပင်လယ်	ko je l pin le
Tasman Sea	တက်စမန်းပင်လယ်	te' sa. man: bin le
Caribbean Sea	ကာရေးဘီးယန်းပင်လယ်	ka rei: bi: jan: bin le
Barents Sea	ဘာရန့်စ် ပင်လယ်	ba jan's bin le
Kara Sea	ကာရာ ပင်လယ်	kara bin le
North Sea	မြောက်ပင်လယ်	mjau' pin le
Baltic Sea	ဘောလ်တစ်ပင်လယ်	bo' l ti' pin le
Norwegian Sea	နော်ဝေးဂျီယန်း ပင်လယ်	no wei: bin le

79. Mountains

mountain	တောင်	taun
mountain range	တောင်တန်း	taun dan:
mountain ridge	တောင်ကြော	taun gjo:
summit, top	ထိပ်	htei'
peak	တောင်ထွတ်	taun htu'
foot (~ of the mountain)	တောင်ခြေ	taun gjei
slope (mountainside)	တောင်စောင်း	taun zaun:
volcano	မီးတောင်	mi: daun
active volcano	မီးတောင်ရှင်	mi: daun shin
dormant volcano	မီးငြိမ်းတောင်	mi: njein: daun

eruption	မီးတောင်ပေါက်ကွဲခြင်း	mi: daun pau' kwe: gjin:
crater	မီးတောင်ဝ	mi: daun wa.
magma	ကျောက်ရည်ပု	kjau' ji bu
lava	ရော်ရည်	cho ji
molten (~ lava)	အရမ်းပူသော	ajam: bu de.

canyon	တောင်ကြားချိုင့်ဝှမ်းနက်	taun gja: gjain. hwan: ne'
gorge	တောင်ကြား	taun gja:
crevice	အက်ကွဲကြောင်း	e' kwe: gjaun:
abyss (chasm)	ချောက်ကမ်းပါး	chau' kan: ba:

pass, col	တောင်ကြားလမ်း	taun gja: lan:
plateau	ကုန်းပြင်မြင့်	koun: bjin mjin:
cliff	ကျောက်ဆောင်	kjau' hsain
hill	တောင်ကုန်း	taun goun:

glacier	ရေခဲမြစ်	jei ge: mji'
waterfall	ရေတံခွန်	jei dan khun
geyser	ရေပူစမ်း	jei bu zan:
lake	ရေကန်	jei gan

plain	မြေပြန့်	mjei bjan:
landscape	ရှုခင်း	shu. gin:
echo	ပဲ့တင်သံ	pe. din than

alpinist	တောင်တက်သမား	taun de' thama:
rock climber	ကျောက်တောင်တက်သမား	kjau' taun de dha ma:
to conquer (in climbing)	အောင်နိုင်သူ	aun nain dhu

| climb (an easy ~) | တောင်တက်ခြင်း | taun de' chin: |

80. Mountains names

The Alps	အဲလ်ပ်တောင်	e.lp daun
Mont Blanc	မောင့်ဘလန့်စ်တောင်	maun. ba. lan. s taun
The Pyrenees	ပိရန်းနီးစ်တောင်	pi jan: ni:s taun

The Carpathians	ကာပသီယန်စ်တောင်	ka pa. dhi jan s taun
The Ural Mountains	ယူရယ်တောင်တန်း	ju re daun dan:
The Caucasus Mountains	ကောကေးဆပ်တောင်တန်း	ko: kei: zi' taun dan:
Mount Elbrus	အယ်ဘရတ်စ်တောင်	e ba. ja's daun

The Altai Mountains	အယ်လတိုင်တောင်	e la. tain daun
The Tian Shan	တိုင်ယန်ရှန်းတောင်	tain jan shin: daun
The Pamir Mountains	ပါမီယာတောင်တန်း	pa mi ja daun dan:
The Himalayas	ဟိမဝန္တာတောင်တန်း	hi. ma. wan da daun dan:
Mount Everest	ဧဝရတ်တောင်	ei wa. ja' taun

| The Andes | အန်ဒီတောင်တန်း | an: di daun dan: |
| Mount Kilimanjaro | ကီလီမန်ဂျာရိုတောင် | ki li man gja gou daun |

81. Rivers

river	မြစ်	mji'
spring (natural source)	စမ်း	san:
riverbed (river channel)	ရေကြောင်းကြောင်း	jei gjo: zi: gjaun:
basin (river valley)	မြစ်ချိုင့်ဝှမ်း	mji' chain. hwan:
to flow into ...	စီးဝင်သည်	si: win de
tributary	မြစ်လက်တက်	mji' le' te'
bank (of river)	ကမ်း	kan:
current (stream)	စီးကြောင်း	si: gaun:
downstream (adv)	ရေရုန့်	jei zoun
upstream (adv)	ရေဆန်	jei zan
inundation	ရေကြီးမှု	jei gji: hmu.
flooding	ရေလျှံခြင်း	jei shan gjin:
to overflow (vi)	လျှံသည်	shan de
to flood (vt)	ရေလွှမ်းသည်	jei hlwan: de
shallow (shoal)	ရေတိမ်ပိုင်း	jei dein bain:
rapids	ရေအောက်ကျောက်ဆောင်	jei au' kjau' hsaun
dam	ဆည်	hse
canal	တူးမြောင်း	tu: mjaun:
reservoir (artificial lake)	ရေလှောင်ကန်	jei hlaun gan
sluice, lock	ရေလွှဲပေါက်	jei hlwe: bau'
water body (pond, etc.)	ရေထု	jei du.
swamp (marshland)	ရွှံ့ညွန့်	shwan njun
bog, marsh	စိမ့်မြေ	sein. mjei
whirlpool	ရေဝဲ	jei we:
stream (brook)	ချောင်းကလေး	chaun: galei:
drinking (ab. water)	သောက်ရေ	thau' jei
fresh (~ water)	ရေချို	jei gjou
ice	ရေခဲ	jei ge:
to freeze over (ab. river, etc.)	ရေခဲသည်	jei ge: de

82. Rivers' names

Seine	ဆိန်းမြစ်	sein mji'
Loire	လောရီမြစ်	lo ji mji'
Thames	သိမ်းမြစ်	thain: mji'
Rhine	ရိုင်းမြစ်	rain: mji'
Danube	ဒိန်နယုမြစ်	din na. ju mji'

Volga	ဗော့လဂါမြစ်	bo la. ga mja'
Don	ဒွန်မြစ်	dun mja'
Lena	လီနာမြစ်	li na mji'

Yellow River	မြစ်ဝါ	mji' wa
Yangtze	ရမ်ဇီးမြစ်	jan zi: mji'
Mekong	မဲခေါင်မြစ်	me: gaun mji'
Ganges	ဂင်္ဂါမြစ်	gan ga. mji'

Nile River	နိုင်းမြစ်	nain: mji'
Congo River	ကွန်ဂိုမြစ်	kun gou mji'
Okavango River	အိုကာဝန်ဂိုမြစ်	ai' hou ban
Zambezi River	ဇမ်ဘီဇီးမြစ်	zan bi zi: mji'
Limpopo River	လင်ပိုပိုမြစ်	lin po pou mji'
Mississippi River	မစ်စစ္စပ်ပီမြစ်	mi' si. si. pi. mji'

83. Forest

| forest, wood | သစ်တော | thi' to: |
| forest (as adj) | သစ်တောနှင့်ဆိုင်သော | thi' to: hnin. zain de. |

thick forest	ထူထပ်သောတော	htu da' te. do:
grove	သစ်ပင်အုပ်	thi' pin ou'
forest clearing	တောတွင်းလဟာပြင်	to: dwin: la. ha bjin

| thicket | ချုံပိတ်ပေါင်း | choun bei' paun: |
| scrubland | ချုံထနောင်းတော | choun hta naun: de. |

| footpath (troddenpath) | လူသွားလမ်းကလေး | lu dhwa: lan: ga. lei: |
| gully | လျို | shou |

tree	သစ်ပင်	thi' pin
leaf	သစ်ရွက်	thi' jwe'
leaves (foliage)	သစ်ရွက်များ	thi' jwe' mja:

fall of leaves	သစ်ရွက်ကြွေခြင်း	thi' jwe' kjwei gjin:
to fall (ab. leaves)	သစ်ရွက်ကြွေသည်	thi' jwe' kjwei de
top (of the tree)	အဖျား	ahpja:

branch	အကိုင်းခွဲ	akain: khwe:
bough	ပင်မကိုင်း	pin ma. gain:
bud (on shrub, tree)	အဖူး	ahpu:
needle (of pine tree)	အပ်နှင့်တူသောအရွက်	a' hnin. bu de. ajwe'
pine cone	ထင်းရှူးသီး	htin: shu: dhi:

tree hollow	အခေါင်းပေါက်	akhaun: bau'
nest	ငှက်သိုက်	hnge' thai'
burrow (animal hole)	မြေတွင်း	mjei dwin:
trunk	ပင်စည်	pin ze
root	အမြစ်	amji'

bark	သစ်ခေါက်	thi' khau'
moss	ရေညို	jei hnji.
to uproot (remove trees or tree stumps)	အမြစ်မှဆွဲနှုတ်သည်	amji' hma zwe: hna' te
to chop down	ခုတ်သည်	khou' te
to deforest (vt)	တောပြုန်းစေသည်	to: bjoun: zei de
tree stump	သစ်ငုတ်တို	thi' ngou' tou
campfire	မီးပုံ	mi: boun
forest fire	မီးလောင်ခြင်း	mi: laun gjin:
to extinguish (vt)	မီးသတ်သည်	mi: tha' de
forest ranger	တောခေါင်း	to: gaun:
protection	သစ်တောဝန်ထမ်း	thi' to: wun dan:
to protect (~ nature)	ထိန်းသိမ်းစောင့်ရှောက်သည်	htein: dhein: zaun. shau' te
poacher	ခိုးယူသူ	khou: ju dhu
steel trap	သံမဏိထောင်ချောက်	than mani. daun gjau'
to gather, to pick (vt)	ရူးသည်	khu: de
to pick (mushrooms)	ဆွတ်သည်	hsu' te
to pick (berries)	ရူးသည်	khu: de
to lose one's way	လမ်းပျောက်သည်	lan: bjau' de

84. Natural resources

natural resources	သဘာဝတ	thajan za da.
minerals	တွင်းထွက်ပစ္စည်း	twin: htwe' pji' si:
deposits	နနး	noun:
field (e.g., oilfield)	ဓာတ်သတ္တုထွက်ရာမြေ	da' tha' tu dwe' ja mjei
to mine (extract)	တူးဖော်သည်	tu: hpo de
mining (extraction)	တူးဖော်ခြင်း	tu: hpo gjin:
ore	သတ္တုရိုင်း	tha' tu. jain:
mine (e.g., for coal)	သတ္တုတွင်း	tha' tu. dwin:
shaft (mine ~)	မိုင်းတွင်း	main: dwin:
miner	သတ္တုတွင်း အလုပ်သမား	tha' tu. dwin: alou' thama:
gas (natural ~)	ဓာတ်ငွေ့	da' ngwei.
gas pipeline	ဓါတ်ငွေ့ပိုက်လိုင်း	da' ngwei. bou' lain:
oil (petroleum)	ရေနံ	jei nan
oil pipeline	ရေနံပိုက်လိုင်း	jei nan bou' lain:
oil well	ရေနံတွင်း	jei nan dwin:
derrick (tower)	ရေနံစင်	jei nan zin
tanker	လောင်စာတင်သင်္ဘော	laun za din dhin bo:
sand	သဲ	the:
limestone	ထုံးကျောက်	htoun: gjau'
gravel	ကျောက်စရစ်	kjau' sa. ji'

89

peat	ဖြေ့ဲ	mjei zwei: ge:
clay	ဖြေး	mjei zei:
coal	ကျောက်မီးသွေး	kjau' mi dhwei:

iron (ore)	သံ	than
gold	ရွှေ	shwei
silver	ငွေ	ngwei
nickel	နီကယ်	ni ke
copper	ကြေးနီ	kjei: ni

zinc	သွပ်	thu'
manganese	မင်္ဂနီစ်	ma' ga. ni:s
mercury	ပြဒါး	bada:
lead	ခဲ	khe:

mineral	သတ္တုများ	tha' tu. za:
crystal	သလင်းကျောက်	thalin: gjau'
marble	စကျင်ကျောက်	zagjin kjau'
uranium	ယူရေနီယမ်	ju rei ni jan

85. Weather

weather	ရာသီဥတု	ja dhi nja. tu.
weather forecast	မိုးလေဝသခန့် မှန်းချက်	mou: lei wa. dha. gan. hman: gje'
temperature	အပူချိန်	apu gjein
thermometer	သာမိုမီတာ	tha mou mi ta
barometer	လေဖိအားတိုင်းကိရိယာ	lei bi. a: dain: gi. ji. ja

| humid (adj) | စိုထိုင်းသော | sou htain: de |
| humidity | စိုထိုင်းမှု | sou htain: hmu. |

heat (extreme ~)	အပူရှိန်	apu shein
hot (torrid)	ပူလောင်သော	pu laun de.
it's hot	ပူလောင်ခြင်း	pu laun gjin:

| it's warm | နွေးခြင်း | nwei: chin: |
| warm (moderately hot) | နွေးသော | nwei: de. |

| it's cold | အေးခြင်း | ei: gjin: |
| cold (adj) | အေးသော | ei: de. |

sun	နေ	nei
to shine (vi)	သာသည်	tha de
sunny (day)	နေသာသော	nei dha de.
to come up (vi)	နေထွက်သည်	nei dwe' te
to set (vi)	နေဝင်သည်	nei win de

| cloud | တိမ် | tein |
| cloudy (adj) | တိမ်ထူသော | tein du de |

| rain cloud | မိုးတိမ် | mou: dain |
| somber (gloomy) | ညို့မိုင်းသော | njou. hmain: de. |

rain	မိုး	mou:
it's raining	မိုးရွာသည်	mou: jwa de.
rainy (~ day, weather)	မိုးရွာသော	mou: jwa de.
to drizzle (vi)	မိုးဖွဲဖွဲ့ရွာသည်	mou: bwe: bwe: jwa de

pouring rain	သည်းထန်စွာရွာသောမိုး	thi: dan zwa jwa dho: mou:
downpour	မိုးပုံဆိန်	mou: bu. zain
heavy (e.g., ~ rain)	မိုးသည်းသော	mou: de: de.
puddle	ရေအိုင်	jei ain
to get wet (in rain)	မိုးမိသည်	mou: mi de

fog (mist)	မြူ	mju
foggy	မြူထူထပ်သော	mju htu hta' te.
snow	နှင်း	hnin:
it's snowing	နှင်းကျသည်	hnin: gja. de

86. Severe weather. Natural disasters

thunderstorm	မိုးသက်မုန်တိုင်း	mou: dhe' moun dain:
lightning (~ strike)	လျှပ်စီး	hlja' si:
to flash (vi)	လျှပ်ပြက်သည်	hlja' pje' te

thunder	မိုးကြိုး	mou: kjou:
to thunder (vi)	မိုးကြိုးပစ်သည်	mou: gjou: pi' te
it's thundering	မိုးကြိုးပစ်သည်	mou: gjou: pi' te

| hail | မိုးသီး | mou: dhi: |
| it's hailing | မိုးသီးကြွေသည် | mou: dhi: gjwei de |

| to flood (vt) | ရေကြီးသည် | jei gji: de |
| flood, inundation | ရေကြီးမှု | jei gji: hmu. |

earthquake	ငလျင်	nga ljin
tremor, shoke	တုန်ခါခြင်း	toun ga gjin:
epicenter	ငလျင်ဗဟိုချက်	nga ljin ba hou che'

| eruption | မီးတောင်ပေါက်ကွဲခြင်း | mi: daun pau' kwe: gjin: |
| lava | ချော်ရည် | cho ji |

twister	လေဆင်နှာမောင်း	lei zin hna maun:
tornado	လေဆင်နှာမောင်း	lei zin hna maun:
typhoon	တိုင်ဖွန်းမုန်တိုင်း	tain hpun moun dain:

hurricane	ဟာရီကိန်းမုန်တိုင်း	ha ji gain: moun dain:
storm	မုန်တိုင်း	moun dain:
tsunami	ဆူနာမိ	hsu na mi
cyclone	ဆိုင်ကလုန်းမုန်တိုင်း	hsain ga. loun: moun dain:

bad weather	ဆိုးရွားေသာ ရာသီဥတု	hsou: jwa: de. ja dhi u. tu.
fire (accident)	မီးေလာင်ခြင်း	mi: laun gjin:
disaster	ေဘးအန္တရာယ်	bei: an daje
meteorite	ဥက္ကာခဲ	ou' ka ge:
avalanche	ေရခဲနှင့်ေကျာက်တုံး များထိုးကျခြင်း	jei ge: hnin kjau' toun: mja: htou: gja. gjin:
snowslide	ေလတိုက်ပြီးဖြစ်ေန ေသာနှင်းပုံ	lei dou' hpji: bi' nei dho: hnin: boun
blizzard	နှင်းမုန်တိုင်း	hnin: moun dain:
snowstorm	နှင်းမုန်တိုင်း	hnin: moun dain:

FAUNA

predator	သားရဲ	tha: je:
tiger	ကျား	kja:
lion	ခြင်္သေ့	chin dhei.
wolf	ဝံပုလွေ	wun bu. lwei
fox	မြေခွေး	mjei gwei:
jaguar	ဂျာကွာကျားသစ်မျိုး	gja gwa gja: dhi' mjou:
leopard	ကျားသစ်	kja: dhi'
cheetah	သစ်ကျွတ်	thi' kjou'
black panther	ကျားသစ်နက်	kja: dhi' ne'
puma	ပျူမားတောင်ခြေသဲ့	pju. ma: daun gjin dhei.
snow leopard	ရေခဲတောင်ကျားသစ်	jei ge: daun gja: dhi'
lynx	လင့်ကြောင်မြီးတို	lin. gjaun mji: dou
coyote	ဝံပုလွေငယ်တစ်မျိုး	wun bu. lwei nge di' mjou:
jackal	ခွေးအ	khwei: a.
hyena	ဟိုင်အီးနား	hain i: na:

animal	တိရစ္ဆာန်	tharei' hsan
beast (animal)	ခြေလေးချောင်းသတ္တဝါ	chei lei: gjaun: dhadawa
squirrel	ရှဉ့်	shin.
hedgehog	ဖြူကောင်	hpju gaun
hare	တောယုန်ကြီး	to: joun gji:
rabbit	ယုန်	joun
badger	ခွေးတူဝက်တူကောင်	khwei: du we' tu gaun
raccoon	ရက်ကွန်းဝံ	je' kwan: wan
hamster	မြီးတိုပါးတွဲကြွက်	mji: dou ba: dwe: gjwe'
marmot	မားမိုတ်ကောင်	ma: mou. t gaun
mole	ပွေး	pwei:
mouse	ကြွက်	kjwe'
rat	မြေကြွက်	mjei gjwe'
bat	လင်းနို့	lin: nou.
ermine	အားမင်ကောင်	a: min gaun
sable	ဆေဘယ်	hsei be

marten	အသားစားအကောင်ငယ်	atha: za: akaun nge
weasel	သားစားဖျံ	tha: za: bjan
mink	မင်ခ်မွေးပါ	min kh mjwei ba
beaver	ဖျံကြီးတစ်မျိုး	hpjan gji: da' mjou:
otter	ဖျံ	hpjan
horse	မြင်း	mjin:
moose	ဦးချိုပြားသော သမင်ကြီး	u: gjou bja: dho: thamin gji:
deer	သမင်	thamin
camel	ကုလားအုပ်	kala: ou'
bison	အမေရိကန်မြေင်	amei ji kan pjaun
wisent	အောရက်စ်	o: re' s
buffalo	ကျွဲ	kjwe:
zebra	မြင်းကျား	mjin: gja:
antelope	အပြေးမြန်သော တောဆိတ်	apjei: mjan de. hto: zei'
roe deer	ဒရယ်ငယ်တစ်မျိုး	da. je nge da' mjou:
fallow deer	ဒရယ်	da. je
chamois	တောင်ဆိတ်	taun zei'
wild boar	တောဝက်ထီး	to: we' hti:
whale	ဝေလငါး	wei la. nga:
seal	ပင်လယ်ဖျံ	pin le bjan
walrus	ဝဲရပ်စ်ဖျံ	wo: ra's hpjan
fur seal	အမွေးပါသောပင်လယ်ဖျံ	amwei: pa dho: bin le hpjan
dolphin	လင်းပိုင်	lin: bain
bear	ဝက်ဝံ	we' wun
polar bear	ဝိုလာဝက်ဝံ	pou la we' wan
panda	ပန်ဒါဝက်ဝံ	pan da we' wan
monkey	မျောက်	mjau'
chimpanzee	ချင်ပင်ဇီမျောက်ဝံ	chin pin zi mjau' wan
orangutan	အောရန်အူတန်လူဝံ	o ran u tan lu wun
gorilla	ဂေါ်ရိလာမျောက်ဝံ	go ji la mjau' wun
macaque	မာကာကွေးမျောက်	ma ga gwei mjau'
gibbon	မျောက်လွှဲကျော်	mjau' hlwe: gjo
elephant	ဆင်	hsin
rhinoceros	ကြံ့	kjan.
giraffe	သစ်ကုလားအုပ်	thi' ku. la ou'
hippopotamus	ရေမြင်း	jei mjin:
kangaroo	သားပိုက်ကောင်	tha: bai' kaun
koala (bear)	ကိုအာလာဝက်ဝံ	kou a la we' wun
mongoose	မြွေပါ	mwei ba
chinchilla	ချင်းချီလာ	chin: chi la
skunk	စကန့်ခ်ဖျံ	sakan. kh hpjan
porcupine	ဖြူ	hpju

89. Domestic animals

cat	ကြောင်	kjaun
tomcat	ကြောင်ထီး	kjaun di:
dog	ခွေး	khwei:
horse	မြင်း	mjin:
stallion (male horse)	မြင်းထီး	mjin: di:
mare	မြင်းမ	mjin: ma.
cow	နွား	nwa:
bull	နွားထီး	nwa: di:
ox	နွားထီး	nwa: di:
sheep (ewe)	သိုး	thou:
ram	သိုးထီး	thou: hti:
goat	ဆိတ်	hsei'
billy goat, he-goat	ဆိတ်ထီး	hsei' hti:
donkey	မြည်း	mji:
mule	လား	la:
pig, hog	ဝက်	we'
piglet	ဝက်ကလေး	we' ka lei:
rabbit	ယုန်	joun
hen (chicken)	ကြက်	kje'
rooster	ကြက်ဖ	kje' pha.
duck	ဘဲ	be:
drake	ဘဲထီး	be: di:
goose	ဘဲငန်း	be: ngan:
tom turkey, gobbler	ကြက်ဆင်	kje' hsin
turkey (hen)	ကြက်ဆင်	kje' hsin
domestic animals	အိမ်မွေးတိရစ္ဆာန်များ	ein mwei: ti. ji. swan mja:
tame (e.g., ~ hamster)	ယဉ်ပါးသော	jin ba: de.
to tame (vt)	ယဉ်ပါးစေသည်	jin ba: zei de
to breed (vt)	သားဖေါက်သည်	tha: bau' te
farm	စိုက်ပျိုးမွေးမြူ ရေးခြံ	sai' pjou: mwei: mju jei: gjan
poultry	ကြက်ဒှက်တိရိစ္ဆန်	kje' ti ji za hsan
cattle	ကျွဲနွားတိရစ္ဆာန်	kjwe: nwa: tarei. zan
herd (cattle)	အုပ်	ou'
stable	မြင်းဇောင်း	mjin: zaun:
pigpen	ဝက်ခြံ	we' khan
cowshed	နွားတင်းကုပ်	nwa: din: gou'
rabbit hutch	ယုန်အိမ်	joun ein
hen house	ကြက်လှောင်အိမ်	kje' hlaun ein

90. Birds

bird	ငှက်	hnge'
pigeon	ခို	khou
sparrow	စာကလေး	sa ga. lei:
tit (great tit)	စာဝတီးငှက်	sa wadi: hnge'
magpie	ငှက်ကျား	hnge' kja:

raven	ကျီးနက်	kji: ne'
crow	ကျီးကန်း	kji: kan:
jackdaw	ဥရောပကျီးတစ်မျိုး	u. jo: pa gji: di' mjou:
rook	ကျီးအ	kji: a.

duck	ဘဲ	be:
goose	ဘဲငန်း	be: ngan:
pheasant	ရစ်ငှက်	ji' hnge'

eagle	လင်းယုန်	lin: joun
hawk	သိမ်းငှက်	thain: hnge'
falcon	အမွဲလိုက်သိမ်းငှက်တစ်မျိုး	ame: lai' thein: hnge' ti' mjou:
vulture	လင်းတ	lin: da.
condor (Andean ~)	တောင်အအမေရိကလင်းတ	taun amei ri. ka. lin: da.

swan	ငန်း	ngan:
crane	ငှက်ကုလား	hnge' ku. la:
stork	ချည်ခင်စွပ်ငှက်	che gin zu' hnge'

parrot	ကြက်တူရွေး	kje: tu jwei:
hummingbird	ငှက်ပိတုန်း	hnge' pi. doun:
peacock	ဥဒေါင်း	u. daun:

ostrich	ငှက်ကုလားအုတ်	hnge' ku. la: ou'
heron	ငဟာင်ငှက်	nga hi' hnge'
flamingo	ကြိုးကြားနီ	kjou: kja: ni
pelican	ငှက်ကြီးဝမ်းပို	hnge' kji: wun bou

| nightingale | တေးဆိုငှက် | tei: hsou hnge' |
| swallow | ပျံလွှား | pjan hlwa: |

thrush	မြေလူးငှက်	mjei lu: hnge'
song thrush	တေးဆိုမြေလူးငှက်	tei: hsou mjei lu: hnge'
blackbird	ငှက်မည်း	hnge' mji:

swift	ပျံလွှားတစ်မျိုး	pjan hlwa: di' mjou:
lark	ဘီလုံးငှက်	bi loun: hnge'
quail	ငုံး	ngoun:

woodpecker	သစ်တောက်ငှက်	thi' tau' hnge'
cuckoo	ဥသြငှက်	udhja hnge'
owl	ဇီးကွက်	zi: gwe

eagle owl	သိမ်းငှက်အနွယ်ဝင်ဗီးကွက်	thain: hnge' anwe win zi: gwe'
wood grouse	ရစ်	ji'
black grouse	ရစ်နက်	ji' ne'
partridge	ခါ	kha

starling	ကျွဲဆက်ရက်	kjwe: hse' je'
canary	စာဝါငှက်	sa wa hnge'
hazel grouse	ရစ်ညို	ji' njou
chaffinch	စာကျွဲခေါင်း	sa gjwe: gaun:
bullfinch	စာကျွဲခေါင်းဂုက်	sa gjwe: gaun: hngwe'

seagull	စင်ဇော်	sin jo
albatross	ပင်လယ်စင်ဇော်ကြီး	pin le zin jo gji:
penguin	ပင်ဂွင်း	pin gwin:

91. Fish. Marine animals

bream	ငါးကြင်းတစ်မျိုး	nga: gjin: di' mjou
carp	ငါးကြင်း	nga: gjin:
perch	ငါးပြမတစ်မျိုး	nga: bjei ma, di' mjou:
catfish	ငါးခူ	nga: gu
pike	ပိုက်ငါး	pai' nga

| salmon | ဆော်လမွန်ငါး | hso: la. mun nga: |
| sturgeon | စတာဂျင်ငါးကြီးမျိုး | sata gjin nga: gji: mjou: |

herring	ငါးသလောက်	nga: dha. lau'
Atlantic salmon	ဆော်လမွန်ငါး	hso: la. mun nga:
mackerel	မက်ကရယ်ငါး	me' ka. je nga:
flatfish	ဥရောပ ငါးဆွေးလျှာတစ်မျိုး	u. jo: pa nga: gwe: sha di' mjou:

zander, pike perch	ငါးပြမအနွယ်ဝင်ငါးတစ်မျိုး	nga: bjei ma. anwe win nga: di' mjou:
cod	ငါးကြီးဆီထုတ်သောငါး	nga: gji: zi dou' de. nga:
tuna	တူနာငါး	tu na nga:
trout	ထရောက်ငါး	hta. jau' nga:

eel	ငါးရှဉ့်	nga: shin.
electric ray	ငါးလက်ထုံ	nga: le' htoun
moray eel	ငါးရှဉ့်ကြီးတစ်မျိုး	nga: shin. gji: da' mjou:
piranha	အသွားစားငါးငယ်တစ်မျိုး	atha. za: nga: nge ti' mjou:

shark	ငါးမန်း	nga: man:
dolphin	လင်းပိုင်	lin: bain
whale	ဝေလငါး	wei la. nga:
crab	ကဏန်း	kanan:
jellyfish	ငါးဖန်ခွက်	nga: hpan gwe'

octopus	ေရဘဝဲ	jei ba. we:
starfish	ကြယ်ငါး	kje nga:
sea urchin	သိပ္ပရုပ်	than ba. gjou'
seahorse	ေရနဂါး	jei naga:

oyster	ကမာေကာင်	kama kaun
shrimp	ပုစွန်	bazun
lobster	ေကျာက်ပုစွန်	kjau' pu. zun
spiny lobster	ေကျာက်ပုစွန်	kjau' pu. zun

92. Amphibians. Reptiles

| snake | ေမြ | mwei |
| venomous (snake) | အဆိပ်ရှိေသာ | ahsei' shi. de. |

viper	ေမြေပွး	mwei bwei:
cobra	ေမြေဟာက်	mwei hau'
python	စပါးအုံးေမြ	saba: oun: mwei
boa	စပါးကြီးေမြ	saba: gji: mwei

grass snake	မြက်ေလျာေမြ	mje' sho: mwei
rattle snake	ခေလာက်ဆွဲေမြ	kha. lau' hswe: mwei
anaconda	အနာကွန်ဒါေမြ	ana kun da mwei

lizard	တွားသွားသတ္တဝါ	twa: dhwa: tha' tawa
iguana	ဖွတ်	hpu'
monitor lizard	ပုတ်သင်	pou' thin
salamander	ေရပုတ်သင်	jei bou' thin
chameleon	ပုတ်သင်ညို	pou' thin njou
scorpion	ကင်းမြီးေကာက်	kin: mji: kau'

turtle	လိပ်	lei'
frog	ဖား	hpa:
toad	ဖားပြုပ်	hpa: bju'
crocodile	မိေကျာင်း	mi. kjaun:

93. Insects

insect, bug	ပိုးမွား	pou: hmwa:
butterfly	လိပ်ပြာ	lei' pja
ant	ပုရွက်ဆိတ်	pu. jwe' hsei'
fly	ယင်ေကာင်	jin gaun
mosquito	ခြင်	chin
beetle	ပိုးေတာင်မာ	pou: daun ma

wasp	နကျယ်ေကာင်	na. gje gaun
bee	ပျား	pja:
bumblebee	ပိတုန်း	pi. doun:

gadfly (botfly)	မှက်	hme'
spider	ပင့်ကူ	pjin. gu
spiderweb	ပင့်ကူအိမ်	pjin gu ein
dragonfly	ပုစဉ်း	bazin
grasshopper	နံကောင်	hnan gaun
moth (night butterfly)	ပိုးဖလံ	pou: ba. lan
cockroach	ပိုးဟပ်	pou: ha'
tick	မှား	hmwa:
flea	သန်း	than:
midge	မှက်အသေးစား	hme' athei: za:
locust	ကျိုင်းကောင်	kjain: kaun
snail	ခရု	khaju.
cricket	ပုရစ်	paji'
lightning bug	ပိုးစုန်းကြူး	pou: zoun: gju:
ladybug	လေဒီဘတ်ပိုးတောင်မာ	lei di ba' pou: daun ma
cockchafer	အုန်းပိုး	oun: bou:
leech	မျှော့	hmjo.
caterpillar	ပေါက်ဖတ်	pau' hpe'
earthworm	တီကောင်	ti gaun
larva	ပိုးတုံးလုံး	pou: doun: loun:

FLORA

94. Trees

tree	သစ်ပင်	thi' pin
deciduous (adj)	ရွက်ပြတ်	jwe' pja'
coniferous (adj)	ထင်းရှူးပင်နှင့်ဆိုင်သော	htin: shu: bin hnin. zain de.
evergreen (adj)	အိဘားဂရင်းပင်	e ba: ga rin: bin
apple tree	ပန်းသီးပင်	pan: dhi: bin
pear tree	သစ်တော်ပင်	thi' to bin
sweet cherry tree	ချယ်ရီသီးအချိုပင်	che ji dhi: akjou bin
sour cherry tree	ချယ်ရီသီးအချဉ်ပင်	che ji dhi: akjin bin
plum tree	ဆီးပင်	hsi: bin
birch	ဘုဇဗတ်ပင်	bu. za. ba' pin
oak	ဝက်သစ်ချပင်	we' thi' cha. bin
linden tree	လင်ဒန်ပင်	lin dan pin
aspen	ပေါ်ပလာပင်တစ်မျိုး	po. pa. la bin di' mjou:
maple	မေပဲပင်	mei pe bin
spruce	ထင်းရှူးပင်တစ်မျိုး	htin: shu: bin ti' mjou:
pine	ထင်းရှူးပင်	htin: shu: bin
larch	ကတော့ပုံထင်းရှူးပင်	ka dau. boun din: shu: pin
fir tree	ထင်းရှူးပင်တစ်မျိုး	htin: shu: bin ti' mjou:
cedar	သစ်ကတိုးပင်	thi' gadou: bin
poplar	ပေါ်ပလာပင်	po. pa. la bin
rowan	ရာအန်ပင်	ra an bin
willow	မိုးမဂပင်	mou: ma. ga. bin
alder	အိုလ်ဒါပင်	oun da bin
beech	ယင်းသစ်	jin: dhi'
elm	အမ်ပင်	an bin
ash (tree)	အက်ရှ်အပင်	e' sh apin
chestnut	သစ်အယ်ပင်	thi' e
magnolia	တတိုင်းဟွေးပင်	ta tain: hmwei: bin
palm tree	ထန်းပင်	htan: bin
cypress	စိုက်ပရက်စ်ပင်	sai' pa. je's pin
mangrove	လမုပင်	la. mu. bin
baobab	ကန္တာရပေါက်ပင်တစ်ချိုး	kan ta ja. bau' bin di' chju:
eucalyptus	ယူကလစ်ပင်	ju kali' pin
sequoia	ဆီကွိုလာပင်	hsi gwou la pin

95. Shrubs

bush	ချုံပုတ်	choun bou'
shrub	ချုံ	choun
grapevine	စပျစ်	zabji'
vineyard	စပျစ်ခြံ	zabji' chan
raspberry bush	ရက်စဘယ်ရှိ	re' sa be ji
blackcurrant bush	ဘလက်ကားရန့်	ba. le' ka: jan.
redcurrant bush	အနီရောင်ဘယ်ရှိသီး	ani jaun be ji dhi:
gooseberry bush	ကုလားဆီးဖြူပင်	kala: zi: hpju pin
acacia	အကေရှားပင်	akei sha: bin:
barberry	ဘားဘယ်ရီပင်	ba: be' ji bin
jasmine	စံပယ်ပင်	san be bin
juniper	ဂျူနီပါပင်	gju ni ba bin
rosebush	နှင်းဆီချုံ	hnin: zi gjun
dog rose	တောရိုင်းနှင်းဆီပင်	to: ein: hnin: zi bin

96. Fruits. Berries

fruit	အသီး	athi:
fruits	အသီးများ	athi: mja:
apple	ပန်းသီး	pan: dhi:
pear	သစ်တော်သီး	thi' to dhi:
plum	ဆီးသီး	hsi: dhi:
strawberry (garden ~)	စတော်ဘယ်ရီသီး	sato be ri dhi:
cherry	ချယ်ရီသီး	che ji dhi:
sour cherry	ချယ်ရီချဉ်သီး	che ji gjin dhi:
sweet cherry	ချယ်ရီချိုသီး	che ji gjou dhi:
grape	စပျစ်သီး	zabji' thi:
raspberry	ရက်စဘယ်ရှိ	re' sa be ji
blackcurrant	ဘလက်ကားရန့်	ba. le' ka: jan.
redcurrant	အနီရောင်ဘယ်ရှိသီး	ani jaun be ji dhi:
gooseberry	ကုလားဆီးဖြူ	ka. la: his: hpju
cranberry	ကရမ်ဘယ်ရှိ	ka. jan be ji
orange	လိမ္မော်သီး	limmo dhi:
mandarin	ပျားလိမ္မော်သီး	pja: lein mo dhi:
pineapple	နာနတ်သီး	na na' dhi:
banana	ငှက်ပျောသီး	hnge' pjo: dhi:
date	စွန်ပလွံသီး	sun palun dhi:
lemon	သံပုရာသီး	than bu. jou dhi:
apricot	တရုတ်ဆီးသီး	jau' hsi: dhi:

peach	မက်မွန်သီး	me' mwan dhi:
kiwi	ကီဝီသီး	ki wi dhi
grapefruit	ဂရိတ်ဖရူသီး	ga. ri' hpa. ju dhi:

berry	ဘယ်ရီသီး	be ji dhi:
berries	ဘယ်ရီသီးများ	be ji dhi: mja:
cowberry	အနီရောင်ဘယ်ရီသီးတစ်မျိုး	ani jaun be ji dhi: di: mjou:
wild strawberry	စတော်ဘယ်ရီရိုင်း	sato be ri jain:
bilberry	ဘီလ်ဘယ်ရီအသီး	bi' l be ji athi:

97. Flowers. Plants

| flower | ပန်း | pan: |
| bouquet (of flowers) | ပန်းစည်း | pan: ze: |

rose (flower)	နှင်းဆီပန်း	hnin: zi ban:
tulip	ကျူးလစ်ပန်း	kju: li' pan:
carnation	ဇော်မွှားပန်း	zo hmwa: bin:
gladiolus	သစ္စာပန်း	thi' sa ban:

cornflower	အပြာရောင်တောပန်းတစ်မျိုး	apja jaun dho ban: da' mjou:
harebell	ခေါင်းရန်းအပြာပန်း	gaun: jan: apja ban:
dandelion	တောပန်းအဝါတစ်မျိုး	to: ban: awa ti' mjou:
camomile	မေမြို့ပန်း	mei. mjou. ban:

aloe	ရှားစောင်းလက်ပတ်ပင်	sha: zaun: le' pa' pin
cactus	ရှားစောင်းပင်	sha: zaun: bin
rubber plant, ficus	ရော်ဘာပင်	jo ba bin

lily	နှင်းပန်း	hnin: ban:
geranium	ကြွေပန်းတစ်မျိုး	kjwei ban: da' mjou:
hyacinth	ဝဒါပန်း	bei da ba:

mimosa	ထိကရုံးကြီးပင်	hti. ga. joun: gji: bin
narcissus	နားဆက်စ်ပင်	na: zi ze's pin
nasturtium	တောင်ကြာကလေး	taun gja galei:

orchid	သစ်ခွပင်	thi' khwa. bin
peony	စန္ဒပန်း	san dapan:
violet	ဝိုင်းအိုးလက်	bain: ou le'

pansy	ပေါင်ဒါပန်း	paun da ban:
forget-me-not	ခင်မမေ့ပန်း	khin ma. mei. pan:
daisy	ဒေစီပန်း	dei zi bin

poppy	ဘိန်းပင်	bin: bin
hemp	ဆေးခြောက်ပင်	hsei: chau' pin
mint	ပူစီနံ	pu zi nan
lily of the valley	နှင်းပန်းတစ်မျိုး	hnin: ban: di' mjou:

snowdrop	နှင်းခေါင်းလောင်းပန်း	hnin: gaun: laun: ban:
nettle	ဖက်ယားပင်	hpe' ja: bin
sorrel	မှော်ချဉ်ပင်	hmjo gji bin
water lily	ကြာ	kja
fern	ဖန်းပင်	hpan: bin
lichen	သစ်ကပ်မှော်	thi' ka' hmo
conservatory (greenhouse)	ဖန်လုံအိမ်	hpan ain
lawn	မြက်ခင်း	mje' khin:
flowerbed	ပန်းစိုက်ခင်း	pan: zai' khan:
plant	အပင်	apin
grass	မြက်	mje'
blade of grass	ရွက်ရှန်း	jwe' chun:
leaf	အရွက်	ajwa'
petal	ပွင့်ချပ်	pwin: gja'
stem	ပင်စည်	pin ze
tuber	ဥမြစ်	u. mi'
young plant (shoot)	အစို့အညှောက်	asou./a hnjau'
thorn	ဆူး	hsu:
to blossom (vi)	ပွင့်သည်	pwin: de
to fade, to wither	ညှိုးနွမ်းသည်	hnjou: nun: de
smell (odor)	အနံ့	anan.
to cut (flowers)	ရိတ်သည်	jei' te
to pick (a flower)	ခူးသည်	khu: de

98. Cereals, grains

grain	နှံစားပင်တို့၏ အစေ့အဆန်	hnan za: bin dou. i. asei. ahsan
cereal crops	ကောက်ပဲသီးနှံ	kau' pe: dhi; nan
ear (of barley, etc.)	အနှံ	ahnan
wheat	ဂျုံဆန်	gja. mei: ka:
rye	ဂျုံရှင်း	gjoun jain:
oats	မြင်းစားဂျုံ	mjin: za: gjoun
millet	ကောက်ပဲသီးနှံပင်	kau' pe: dhi: nan bin
barley	မုယောစပါး	mu. jo za. ba:
corn	ပြောင်းဖူး	pjaun: bu:
rice	ဆန်စပါး	hsan zaba
buckwheat	ပန်းဂျုံ	pan: gjun
pea plant	ပဲစေ့	pe: zei.
kidney bean	စိုလ်စားပဲ	bou za: be:
soy	ပဲပုပ်ပဲ	pe: bou' pe
lentil	ပဲနီကလေး	pe: ni ga. lei:
beans (pulse crops)	ပဲအမျိုးမျိုး	pe: amjou: mjou:

COUNTRIES OF THE WORLD

99. Countries. Part 1

Afghanistan	အာဖဂန်နစ္စတန်	apha. gan na' tan
Albania	အယ်လ်ဘေးနီးယား	e l bei: ni: ja:
Argentina	အာဂျင်တီးနား	agin ti: na:
Armenia	အာမေးနီးယား	a me: ni: ja:
Australia	ဩစတြေးလျ	thja za djei: lja
Austria	ဩစတြီးယား	o. sa. tji: ja:
Azerbaijan	အာဇာဘိုင်ဂျန်း	a za bain gjin:
The Bahamas	ဘာဟာမက်	ba ha me'
Bangladesh	ဘင်္ဂလားဒေ့ရှ်	bang la: dei. sh
Belarus	ဘီလာရုစ်	bi la ju'
Belgium	ဘယ်လ်ဂျီယံ	be l gji jan
Bolivia	ဘိုလစ်ဗီးယား	bou la' bi: ja:
Bosnia and Herzegovina	ဘော့စ်နီးယားနှင့်ဟာ ဇီဂိုဗီနာ	bo'. ni: ja: hnin. ha zi gou bi na
Brazil	ဘရာဇီလ်	ba. ra zi'l
Bulgaria	ဘူလ်ဂေးရီးယား	bou gei: ji: ja
Cambodia	ကမ္ဘောဒီးယား	ga khan ba di: ja:
Canada	ကနေဒါနိုင်ငံ	ka. nei da nain gan
Chile	ချီလီ	chi li
China	တရုတ်	tajou'
Colombia	ကိုလမ်းဘီးယား	kou lan: bi: ja:
Croatia	ခရိုအေးရှား	kha. jou ei: sha:
Cuba	ကျူးဘား	kju: ba:
Cyprus	ဆူးပရက်စ်	hsu: pa. je' s te.
Czech Republic	ချက်	che'
Denmark	ဒိန်းမတ်	dein: ma'
Dominican Republic	ဒိုမီနီကန်	dou mi ni kan
Ecuador	အီကွေဒေါ	i kwei: do:
Egypt	အီဂျစ်	igji'
England	အင်္ဂလန်	angga. lan
Estonia	အက်စ်တိုးနီးယား	e's to' ni: ja:
Finland	ဖင်လန်	hpin lan
France	ပြင်သစ်	pjin dhi'
French Polynesia	ပြင်သစ် ပေါ်လီးနီးရှား	pjin dhi' po li: ni: sha:
Georgia	ဂျော်ဂျီယာ	gjo gji ja
Germany	ဂျာမန်	gja man
Ghana	ဂါနာ	ga na
Great Britain	အင်္ဂလန်	angga. lan

Greece	ဂရိ	ga. ri.
Haiti	ဟိုင်တီ	hain ti
Hungary	ဟန်ဂေရီ	han gei ji

100. Countries. Part 2

Iceland	အိုက်စလန်း	ai' sa lan:
India	အိန္ဒိယ	indi. ja
Indonesia	အင်ဒိုနီးရှား	in do ni: sha:
Iran	အီရန်	iran
Iraq	အီရတ်	ira'
Ireland	အိုင်ယာလန်	ain ja lan
Israel	အစ္စရေး	a' sa. jei:
Italy	အီတလီ	ita. li
Jamaica	ဂျမေးကား	g'me:kaa:
Japan	ဂျပန်	gja pan
Jordan	ဂျော်ဒန်	gjo dan
Kazakhstan	ကာဇက်စတန်	ka ze' satan
Kenya	ကင်ညာ	kin nja
Kirghizia	ကစ်ရီကစ္စတန်	ki' ji ki' za. tan
Kuwait	ကူဝိတ်	ku wi'
Laos	လာအို	la ou
Latvia	လတ်ဗီယန်	la' bi jan
Lebanon	လက်ဘနွန်	le' ba. nun
Libya	လီဗီယာ	li bi ja
Liechtenstein	ဗာတီကန်လူမျိုး	ba di gan dhu mjo:
Lithuania	လစ်သူနီယံ	li' thu ni jan
Luxembourg	လျူဆန်ဘော့	lju hsan bo.
Macedonia (Republic of ~)	မက်ဆီဒိုးနီးယား	me' hsi: dou: ni: ja:
Madagascar	မာဒက်ကာစကာ	ma de' ka za ga
Malaysia	မလေးရှား	ma. lei: sha:
Malta	မာတာ	ma ta
Mexico	မက္ကဆီကို နိုင်ငံ	me' ka. hsi kou nain ngan
Moldova, Moldavia	မိုဒိုရာ	mou dou ja
Monaco	မိုနာကို	mou na kou
Mongolia	မွန်ဂိုလီးယား	mun gou li: ja:
Montenegro	မွန်တန်နီဂရို	mun dan ni ga. jou
Morocco	မော်ရိုကို	mo jou gou
Myanmar	မြန်မာ	mjan ma
Namibia	နမ်မီးဘီးယား	nami: bi: ja:
Nepal	နီပေါ	ni po:
Netherlands	နယ်သာလန်	ne dha lan
New Zealand	နယူးဇီလန်	na. ju: zi lan
North Korea	မြောက်ကိုရီးယား	mjau' kou ji: ja:
Norway	နော်ဝေး	no wei:

101. Countries. Part 3

Pakistan	ပါကစ္စတန်	pa ki' sa. tan
Palestine	ပါလက်စတိုင်း	pa le' sa tain:
Panama	ပနားမား	pa. na: ma:
Paraguay	ပါရာဂွေး	pa ja gwei:
Peru	ပီရူး	pi ju:
Poland	ပိုလန်	pou lan
Portugal	ပေါ်တူဂီ	po tu gi
Romania	ရူမေးနီးယား	ru mei: ni: ja:
Russia	ရုရှား	ru. sha:
Saudi Arabia	ဆော်ဒီအာရေဗီးယား	hso: di a jei. bi: ja:
Scotland	စကော့တလန်	sa. ko: talan
Senegal	ဆယ်နီဂေါ်	hse ni go
Serbia	ဆယ်ဗီယန်	hse bi jan.
Slovakia	ဆလိုဗားကီးယာ	hsa. lou ba ki ja
Slovenia	ဆလိုဗီးနီးယား	hsa. lou bi ni: ja:
South Africa	တောင်အာဖရိက	taun a hpa. ji. ka.
South Korea	တောင်ကိုရီးယား	taun kou ri: ja:
Spain	စပိန်	sapein
Suriname	ဆူရီနိမ်း	hsu. ji nei:
Sweden	ဆွီဒင်	hswi din
Switzerland	ဆွစ်ဇာလန်	hswa' za lan
Syria	ဆီးရီးယား	hsi: ji: ja:
Taiwan	ထိုင်ဝမ်	htain wan
Tajikistan	တာဂျစ်ကစ္စတန်	ta gji' ki' sa. tan
Tanzania	တန်ဇားနီးယား	tan za: ni: ja:
Tasmania	တာ့စ်မေးနီးယား	ta. s mei: ni: ja:
Thailand	ထိုင်း	htain:
Tunisia	တူနစ်ရှား	tu ni' sha:
Turkey	တူရကီ	tu ra. ki
Turkmenistan	တာ့ပ်မင်နစ္စတန်	ta' min ni' sa. tan
Ukraine	ယူကရိန်း	ju ka. jein:
United Arab Emirates	အာရပ်နိုင်ငံများ	a ra' nain ngan mja:
United States of America	အမေရိကန် ပြည်ထောင်စု	amei ji kan pji htaun zu
Uruguay	အူရုဂွေး	ou. ju gwei:
Uzbekistan	ဥဇဘက်ကစ္စတန်	u. za. be' ki' sa. tan
Vatican	ဘာတိကန်	ba di gan
Venezuela	ဗယ်နီဇွဲလား	be ni zwe: la:
Vietnam	ဗီယက်နမ်	bi je' nan
Zanzibar	ဇန်ဇီဘာ	zan zi ba

www.ingramcontent.com/pod-product-compliance
Lightning Source LLC
Chambersburg PA
CBHW070815050426
42452CB00011B/2058